Personal
Bible
Study

Dr. Emmert

Sept. 17 NO CLASS
oct. 6 NO CLASS   " 24
   " 8

nov. 3   oct 27 NO CLASS
   DAYOFPRAYER   " 29

nov. 10
   PRESIDENTS
      DAY

(1-207-442-7444)

Personal Bible Study

William C. Lincoln

 Bethany Fellowship INC.
MINNEAPOLIS, MINNESOTA 55438

Quotations on the facer pages of each chapter are taken from
The Annotated Sherlock Holmes by William S. Baring-Gould,
copyright © 1967 by Lucille M. Baring-Gould. Used by permission
of Crown Publishers, Inc.

Published by Bethany Fellowship, Inc.
6820 Auto Club Road, Minneapolis, Minnesota 55438

Printed in the United States of America

Library of Congress Cataloging in Publication Data:

Lincoln, William C   1926-
    Personal Bible study.

    Bibliography: p.
    1. Bible—Study. I. Title.
BS600.2.L44   220'.07   75-2345
ISBN 0-87123-458-0

*Dedicated
to my father, Arthur B. Lincoln,
who, throughout my boyhood, taught me,
by precept and by example,
to LIVE and LOVE the Word of God*

Table of Contents

Preface to the Second Edition

This manual has been in use now for three years, during which time it has been possible to observe the response of students to it. Many helpful suggestions have come from those who have used it, and every attempt has been made to seriously consider each one and to make those changes that seem beneficial to a clear understanding of the inductive method.

Several paragraphs have been rewritten and some new material has been added for illustrative purposes. In addition, we have sought to develop a little more sharply the analogy between Bible study and the work of the detective. If only we can learn to search diligently for the clues and to carefully observe them, our understanding of the Scriptures will be enhanced.

Preface

In 1951 I was asked to begin teaching part time at the Northeastern Bible College, while continuing to serve as pastor of the Englewood Baptist Temple in Englewood, New Jersey. In 1956 I resigned my pastorate to devote myself full time to preparing young people for the ministry of the Word of God. Originally I was to teach Church History and Greek, but soon other courses were added. Among them was a course in hermeneutics, or "How to Study the Bible."

I was a graduate of a moderately conservative theological seminary and considered myself a sound biblical preacher. But I came to truly love the Word of God through a year of study at the then Biblical Seminary of New York. I shall always be grateful for the inspiration of several members of the faculty, including Dr. Emily Werner and Dr. Robert A. Traina. When I was asked to teach hermeneutics, I determined that I would try to communicate to the students something of the challenge and thrill of firsthand study of the Scriptures that I had received from their classes.

In 1952 Dr. Traina published his book, *Methodical Bible Study*, and immediately we began to use it as a text. For twenty years we have continued to do so, but with the growing conviction that something was needed on the undergraduate level to challenge young people in Bible colleges not to be satisfied with 'secondhand' Bible truth. The results of this growing conviction are recorded in this manual.

In addition to those already mentioned, I would like to express my deep appreciation for the encouragement and support of the Rev. James G. Kallam, Dean of Northeastern and my colleague through these years in seeking to communicate the thrill of inductive Bible study to students. For a number of years we have 'team-taught' a senior seminar in Bible study method, and had hoped to collaborate on a book that would capture our mutual concerns. Unfortunately, Mr. Kallam's increasing administrative responsibilities made this impossible. Instead, he kindly relieved me of teaching responsibilities during one summer session in order to make it possible to complete this work.

I would like to express my thanks also to Mrs. Helen Wang for her faithful and diligent work in typing the copy, and to Mr. Charles Irons for his work in producing the finished product.

In my quoting of Scripture, I have usually used the *New American Standard Bible* (NASB), although occasionally I have used the King James and the Revised Version of 1901.

This work is sent forth with the earnest prayer that young men and women will learn not only to *know* the Word of God, but also to *love* the Word of God, which is much more important.

William C. Lincoln

Introduction

You have been out with your family for the evening. When you arrive home and drive up to the house, it is 10:45 p.m. As you put your key in the lock, somehow a feeling of apprehension grips you. The door opens, you switch on the light—and gasp! The entire house seems to be in shambles! Drawers are overturned and emptied on the floor; the furniture is in disarray. As you rush from room to room you wonder, "Whatever was the matter with Baron? Why didn't he bark and frighten them away? Where is he now?" And then you find him: there he lies, between the kitchen and the pantry, his head crushed by a cruel blow—the lovely German shepherd that had been practically a member of the family for five years!

As soon as you get hold of yourself a bit, you rush to the telephone and dial the police. An irritatingly calm voice takes down your name, address, and the salient facts of what has apparently happened and then, with a firm note of authority, says, "Some officers will be there in a few moments. *Please, do not touch anything!*"

Why does he give this last instruction? After all, if some strange men are coming, you ought to tidy up a bit! The place is a mess! Surely, you can describe the way things were! But somehow the authority of that voice restrains you.

When the officers come, you understand. They proceed to examine everything very carefully and see things that you never saw. They are trained to observe clues, to see everything!

What we seek to do in this manual is to train Bible students to be like those detectives: to see everything, to observe *all* the clues, and to arrive at the truth.

The analogy is not nearly as farfetched as it might seem. The principles of induction—observing every detail, asking questions, researching clues, drawing tentative conclusions, arriving at truth—are surely applicable in both instances.

Sherlock Holmes, in his patient guidance of his constant companion, Dr. Watson, illustrates for us the basic principles of induction. We shall attempt to use some of his statements to underscore our points as we move along through our manual.

"... I was always oppressed with a sense of my own stupidity in my dealings with Sherlock Holmes. Here I had heard what he had heard, I had seen what he had seen, and yet from his words it was evident that he saw clearly not only what had happened, but what was about to happen, while to me the whole business was still confused and grotesque."

—The Redheaded League

CHAPTER 1

The Proper Approach

Pick up your Bible and hold it in your hand. Now, ask yourself, "What is it that I am holding?" The answer to that question, not the verbalized answer but the honest response of a life commitment, will determine whether or not you are ready to learn how to study it.

"Well, it is a book," you say. Correct. We therefore conclude that we must study it as we would study any book, considering various laws of literary structure and usage, analyzing vocabulary and thought patterns with the end in view of developing a thorough understanding of what the author is saying.

"But wait," you hasten to add; "it is more like a collection of books. There are a number of different authors and varied writing styles." Correct again. Each of these books, then, must be studied individually, taking into account that different authors will have different ways of expressing themselves. Naturally, we will want to determine what it is that has led to the gathering together of these books. Why have they been grouped together in this fashion? But first, we must learn what the individual books have to say.

"Of course, it is called the *Holy* Bible. It is believed to be the Word of God." The words sound rather 'pious' and perhaps your hesitation betrays something of your lack of conviction at this point. Do *you* believe that this book is the Word of God? Your answer here is very basic! If you are really ready to stake your life on the fact that this written book which you now hold in your hand is the Word of God to man (and this is what it means to 'believe' anything; if you are not willing to stake your life on it, you don't really believe it), then you are ready to proceed with this book and learn the basic techniques of studying the Bible. In the following pages we do not intend to prove that the Bible is the Word of God; that is not the purpose of the present work. But if you are to profit from this study, you must believe the Bible *is* the Word of God with fervent conviction. The evidences abound that support such a conviction, and it is the starting point for a careful and devoted study of the Scriptures.

Consider the implications: (1) Since this book is the Word of God, it means that God has chosen to reveal himself and His program for mankind in a manner that makes it possible for you to study and learn more and more of Him and what He is doing in the world.

(2) Since this book is the Word of God, it surely is the most important book in all of your library, indeed in all the libraries of the world. No book can even approach its relevance to you and your life and future. It is certainly more significant to discover what God thinks of your behavior and your plans than it is to study the philosophies of all men put together.

(3) Since this book is the Word of God, it means that you are not left to depend upon fleeting visions

of dreams in the night to determine what God wants you to do. It is not some subjective experience that guides you; it is a written record to which you can return again and again for reassurance and further enlightenment.

(4) Since this book is the Word of God, it is worth all the effort that you might expend in seeking to learn its truths. There is no work that is too tedious, no assignment too burdensome, no effort too great when you consider that the result will be a better understanding of what God is saying to you.

Yes, that's right: what God is saying *to you.* It is not only that we must believe that the Bible is the Word of God to men; we must believe it is the Word of God *"to me."* He is communicating directly to *you* through this book. It has been suggested that one could compare the Scriptures to a personal letter from his best friend. Do you remember how you devoured that last letter from your sweetheart? You weighed every word, studied every sentence, re-read every paragraph. You tried your best to "read between the lines" to determine how the author felt when the words were recorded. But surely the love that exists between the Lord and His children is far greater than any human love; should we not recognize that His 'letter' to us deserves the same devoted attention?

All right, we have established that the Bible is the Word of God to you. Now, how do you go about studying it? Let us consider first some of the common ways in which people approach the Scriptures:

(1) *The consultation approach*: "I have a problem; I must find out what the Bible has to say about it." There are many folks who use their Bible in the same way they use their medical dictionary! What is the cure for my spiritual ills? Discouraged? Try

this verse. Lonely? Look at this text. The tragedy of this use of the Scripture is that when we are really in desperate need, we don't know where to look because the book is too unfamiliar to us.

(2) *The vitamin pill approach*: "A few verses a day supplies the needed spiritual strength for the Christian life." This approach, unfortunately, can degenerate into almost a "rabbit's foot talisman" defense against life's problems.

(3) *The consecutive approach*: "A chapter a day keeps Satan away." If we limit ourselves to this method, we rob ourselves of an opportunity to really grasp the meaning of the Scriptures. The chapter divisions in our text are very arbitrary. They were not in the original writings and often seriously interrupt the flow of thought. This, of course, is even more serious when we limit our reading to a text divided into verses. Our text should be divided into paragraphs, the basic unit of literary thought, and we should be on the alert constantly to see relationships between the paragraphs. This is extremely difficult when we read the word 'chapter' as though it were spelled 'stop'!

(4) *The repetition approach*: "Every Christian should read through the Bible every year." Correct. This is at least the basic exposure that each Christian should have to the Word of God in its entirety. However, this is not the way to *study* the Bible. While we certainly should read the Scriptures each year, we do not therefore conclude that we are absorbing all the truths that are contained in it.

(5) *The devotional commentary approach*: "Learn what the Scripture says by reading what the experts have to say about it." Certainly, we can profit from what others have to say, but we need to be careful not to see the Scriptures through the prej-

udices of someone else. Remember, this is God's message to *you.* Do you ask someone else to interpret your personal letters? God is anxious for you to read, study and learn the truths of Scripture for yourself.

Well, then, what is the correct approach to follow? What is the proper way to study the Word of God? The following pages will develop an approach which might be entitled the *methodical inductive approach* to the study of the Scriptures.[1] Let us consider the meaning of these terms.

When we say that the correct way to come to an understanding of the Bible is through an *inductive* approach, we mean that you should do it *yourself.* Look at all the data in the passage and determine for yourself what it means. Just as a detective studies the scene of a crime to gather clues as to what actually happened, so the individual student examines all the relevant material that he has to seek to uncover the truth of the passage.

In the field of logic, inductive reasoning is contrasted with deductive reasoning. In deduction, the philosopher begins with established laws, or truths, that he holds as basic premises, and draws conclusions from them. It has often been pointed out that you can prove just about anything by deduction. For example, would you like to prove to your sweetheart that she loves you? Simple. Try this:

> Basic premise: All the world loves a lover.
> I love you; therefore I am a lover.
> You are part of the world; therefore, you love me.

We do not mean to suggest that the Bible student should never use deduction. The real problem is in establishing the truth of the basic premise. Without going into details that belong to the study of logic, suffice it to say here that one should establish *truth* by the process of *induction*, and then use *deductive* reasoning to *elicit the implications* of that truth for life. In the present study, deduction is reserved for the final step—when we *apply* what we have found.

If deduction is the basic method of the philosopher, one might suggest that induction is the root of the so-called scientific method. The scientist seeks to establish all the facts concerning a matter before he draws conclusions. He begins by carefully observing all of the relevant phenomena and recording the results of his study; he then thoughtfully seeks to put the pieces together and develops a theory or hypothesis (or 'guess') as to what causes the particular situation being studied. Next he proceeds to test his theory and either reinforces it or excludes it on the basis of further research.

When you consult a physician, his first concern is to make a thorough examination of your condition. By testing your vital processes (temperature, blood pressure, etc.) and by asking you various questions concerning how you feel, he gradually develops a diagnosis of what is wrong with you. He then proceeds to test his diagnosis by determining whether there are further evidences of the presence of a particular condition. If he confirms the diagnosis, he establishes a pattern of treatment based upon his prior knowledge of the way in which the human body may be treated for that particular illness.

What we are suggesting, then, is that you as a student of the Scriptures should study all of the relevant data for yourself. As a Christian you have the Holy Spirit residing in you. Jesus promised that He would "guide you into all truth" (John 16:13). Part of the ministry of the Holy Spirit, then, is to guide you as you seek to determine the meaning of the

Word of God. As you read and study, He provides the illumination to enable you to correctly interpret the Scriptures.

But, come back to the title of our approach. It is not only *inductive*; it is also *methodical*. There are definite and distinct steps to be followed. Perhaps the classic definition of method is that given by John Dewey in the *Cyclopedia of Education*:

> Method at bottom is but the way of doing things followed in any given case.... The main steps that have to be taken ... and the crucial points where conditions of growth have to be carefully maintained and fostered.[2]

When applied to Bible study then, we might say that

> Methodical Bible study ... is concerned with the proper path to be taken in order to arrive at Scriptural truth. More specifically, it involves the discovery of those steps necessary for achieving its goal and their arrangement in a logical and effective manner.[3]

When one seeks to develop his ability to interpret the Scriptures, he is concerned with increasing his *skill* to do so. Compare it with any skill, such as playing a musical instrument, competing in a sport, learning to swim; the analogies are almost endless. In order to do these things you must learn basic steps to be taken one after the other; you must concentrate on mastering lesser skills in order to perform the complete skill adequately; you play the scales before you try the sonatas. And then, you *practice* constantly. After everything is said and done, your lifelong practice of this method will determine whether or not you will become an adequate student and teacher of the Word of God.

Professor H. H. Horne in a book entitled *Psycho-*

logical Principles of Education records for us what he feels are the five points where *method* breaks down. As we look at these we can see five areas of potential weakness in any methodical approach to the study of the Word of God.

First, he suggests that there might be a *lack of observation*. The expert detective is the one that *sees* what others fail to see. To Sherlock Holmes it may be "elementary, my dear Watson"; but that was because he trained himself to see the details that others overlooked. In our study of the Scriptures we must discipline ourselves to see what is on the page.

Secondly, Professor Horne warns us against a *lack of reflection*. We must learn to develop efficiency in our thinking. When we put the two facts together and draw conclusions, they must be valid. (When two and two do not add up to four, we had better look again at our data!) Thinking is hard work, but it is essential if we are to interpret the Scriptures.

Thirdly, we are constantly in danger of developing a *mental dependence upon others*. It is fairly easy to accept the views of a popular professor or to be swayed by the dogmatic assertions of a strong personality. Remember that because someone else says it is so just does not constitute enough authority. Can you substantiate it in the Scriptures for yourself?

In the fourth place, method can break down because of *prejudice*. Whatever you 'prejudge' before you look at the facts has been decided by prejudice. Every one of us is prejudiced; it is important for us to know our prejudices and seek to overcome their negative pull by intensive study of the scriptural evidence.

It was Huxley who wrote, "Sit down before fact

as a little child; be prepared to give up every pre-
conceived notion, follow humbly and to whatever
abysses nature leads, or you shall learn nothing."

The last warning that Professor Horne gives us
as to how method may break down is that we may
fail through *lack of experience*. Does this mean that
we should give up before we start? "After all," you
say, "I have never had any experience." But there
is only one way to learn how to do a thing and that
is to *do* it. You will never learn to play tennis by
reading a manual on the sport; you must get out
on the court and practice. You will never learn to
play the piano by listening to someone else and wish-
ing; you must take lessons, exercise the scales, and
work, work, work. So it is in Bible study. We will seek
to give you the principles that we feel are basic to
the mastery of the skill; but you must *do* it.

"The ideal reasoner . . . would, when he has once been shown a single fact in all of its bearings, deduce from it not only all the chain of events which led up to it, but also all the results which would follow from it . . . The observer who has thoroughly understood one link in a series of incidents should be able accurately to state all the other ones, both before and after."
—The Five Orange Pips

CHAPTER 2

Examining the Data: Seeing the Whole

We have seen the importance of doing the study ourselves; and we have recognized that it is important that we have a *method*, a procedure that should be followed step-by-step to accomplish our goal. We now turn our attention to the details of the method. What is it that we should do? What are the steps to be followed in order to adequately study and interpret the written text of the Scriptures.

In the subsequent pages of this book we will be suggesting that we must first *examine the data*, looking from the whole to the parts and then from the parts to the whole. Secondly, we must *question the data*, seeking to consider every facet of the passage. Then we should *interpret the data*, using sound principles to determine the meaning of the material. Here we find answers to our questions, summarize what we have found, and seek to recreate the passage so as to be able to develop a comprehensive grasp of the work under consideration. Our fourth step is to *test the data* by looking at its relationship to other passages of the Scriptures. Finally, it is very important to *apply the data*, both to our own lives and to the lives of those to whom we present the

Word: our Sunday school class, our congregation, our family, or whoever.

① Read the Book

We are now ready to begin. What is the very first thing to do when we determine to study a book of the Bible? The answer is so obvious that it will seem trite: we must *read* it. It is astonishing how often people seek to interpret the Word of God by just reading a paragraph, or a few verses, and waxing eloquent as to what that paragraph or those few verses mean. It is impossible to understand the book without reading it in its entirety.

It is important to remind ourselves that we are not to read it piecemeal, a little at a time. Any book that we are studying should be read in its entirety, preferably at one sitting. One marvels at the number of born-again Christians who have never done this! With the exception of the few one-chapter books (Obadiah, Philemon, 2 and 3 John, Jude), the majority of believers have never read a book from beginning to end. We will use the term 'unit-read' for this process.

How long does it take? With the exception of the book of Psalms, which involves some special procedures, our longest book is Isaiah. It has sixty-six chapters and will constitute fifty or sixty pages in the average Bible. Conceivably it might take an average reader three or four hours to read this book at one sitting. Admittedly this might be difficult, but the effort is worthwhile for the benefits gained. If one cannot unit-read the complete book, he should certainly read as much as possible and seek to finish it in no more than two sittings. Remember that most of our books are considerably shorter than this and can be read from start to finish.

Perhaps you are wondering if this is really so important. You will not become sensitive to the flow of the book or the argument of the author unless you become conscious of it as a unified whole. The author did not write in chapters; even when the book is a compilation of messages given on varied occasions, the gathering together of the messages has been done with some clear purpose in mind.

Several hints might help you here. (1) Be sure to use a text that is written in paragraph form. Most Christians have a deep love for the *King James* Bible, often called the *Authorized Version*; but if your copy is divided into verses, it will be extremely difficult, if not impossible, for you to follow the author's train of thought. The basic unit of literary expression is the paragraph; each paragraph seeks to present the development of a single idea. A paragraph text is better suited for a study Bible.

(2) Use a text that is written in contemporary English. Words have a way of changing in their meaning with the passage of time. Consider, for example, Romans 1:13 in the King James text, where Paul says, "Oftentimes I purposed to come unto you, (but was *let* hitherto,) . . . " The word 'let' meant "to hinder" in the early seventeenth century when the King James text was written. What does it mean today? It means "to permit"! Here is an example of a word completely reversing its meaning in usage. As another example, Paul says in Philippians 1:27, "Only let your *conversation* be as it becometh the gospel of Christ." What does the word 'conversation' mean to you? It denotes your talk with another person, the exchange of verbal ideas. But when the text was translated, the word meant the totality of behavior. Paul here is urging us to have the total pattern of our lives such that we do not disgrace the

gospel. Words change, and therefore we should work with a text that uses an up-to-date vocabulary.

(3) On the whole, it is wiser to use a text that has been developed by a group of scholars rather than to use the translation of a single man. Thus, while the English usage of a New Testament like Weymouth's is beautiful, it is probably preferable to use one that has been developed by several authorities. The *Revised Standard Version* reveals some doctrinal bias towards liberalism, but it is basically a competent translation. The *American Standard Version* of 1901 is good, but the paragraph divisions tend to be rather unwieldy and long. The *New American Standard Bible* (NASB) is one of the best texts available. Unfortunately, for some strange reason, the translators returned to a versification of the text. *The New English Bible* has many good points; certainly it is in up-to-date English idiom. It is felt by some, however, to be rather free in its rendering of the original texts. *The Modern Language Bible* (the New Berkeley Version) is a very fine text. Another that should be considered is the translation currently being developed as *The New International Version*. At this writing it is available only in the New Testament. These last two are the product of fine evangelical scholarship. Perhaps the best suggestion is to secure a copy of all of these and gain the benefit of varied translations and insights.

(4) Don't be satisfied with just one reading. You need to expose yourself to the content of the text as fully as possible. Read and reread and reread. One of the greatest of expository preachers and teachers in this century was Dr. G. Campbell Morgan of England. In 1933, Dr. Morgan wrote:

> I have always advocated that beginners should commence with the New Testament and get a bird's

eye view of each book, the simplest method being taking a book, say the Gospel of Matthew, and reading it straight through at a sitting, and *doing this repeatedly until the general movement of the book is grasped.*[1]

The first step of his method of Bible study was the simple reading process. He testified, "I think my analyses of books are the result of having read them on an average of forty to fifty times."[2]

Students are often overwhelmed at the thought of repeated rereadings. The reaction is often, "I just don't have the time!" Here we come again to the question of priorities. If we are convinced that the Bible is the Word of God, we should be ready for any method that will enable us to understand it better. Some techniques may be difficult to learn, but we can *all* read and reread. Of course, the amount of time and effort we put in for any particular course or book will depend on the time that we have. In this, as in everything, the Lord does not expect us to do more than we can. He just asks our *best*!

Now, let us consider what it is we are looking for as we proceed with these readings. Back in 1940, Mortimer J. Adler wrote a book that became practically a classic in the field of reading, *How to Read a Book.* In suggesting the procedure for reading properly, he said that it is important to move from the whole book to the parts. In this reading you must know—

> (1) what kind of book it is; that is, the subject matter it is about. You must also know (2) what the book as a whole is trying to say; (3) into what parts the whole is divided, and (4) what the main problems are that the author is trying to solve.[3]

Consider, then, how this would apply to Bible study.

2. See the Whole

(1) *Categorize the book.* What is the area of subject matter with which the particular book being studied deals? For example, as you read the book of Acts, you note that you are concerned with selected accounts of a historical record of the development of the church from its beginning through the missionary journeys of Paul. It is, therefore, categorized as *history.* In reading the book of Exodus you note that you are studying an account of the leading of the people of Israel out of Egypt into the wilderness, and the giving of the Law at Mount Sinai: again, history. In contrast, the epistle of Paul to the Philippians would be categorized as a letter from Paul to the church at Philippi. (Remember, the word 'epistle' means "letter.") Other possible categories are: *poetry* (as the book of Psalms); *law* (as in the latter part of Exodus and Leviticus); *prophecy* (as in the latter portion of Daniel); *apocalypse* (as in Zechariah); *biography* (as in the Gospel narratives); *story* (as in the book of Ruth).

It is interesting to note that the Jews had three categories for their Old Testament: The *law,* the *prophets,* and the *writings.*

It can readily be seen that a given book might contain material that would suggest more than one category, but it is probably helpful to decide which category would encompass the greater portion of the book. One would not categorize Isaiah as poetry, even though it has some poetic sections.

(2) *Epitomize the book.* The first step has not accomplished its purpose until you can state the theme of the entire book in a very brief statement. This enables you to grasp the overall picture of the book. This is not the same as the previous point, despite its seeming similarity. In the first instance, your con-

cern is to classify the book among the potential kinds of books that one might read, for instance, a historical account, a biography, a letter, etc. Here your concern is with the particular book: What is the overall theme of *this* work? Your grasp of this provides the backdrop for all of your subsequent study of the work. Continue your unit-reading until you are able to state what the entire book is saying in one or two sentences.

(3) *Compartmentalize the book.* It is very important for you to see the structure of the book. What are its major divisions? How do they, in turn, break down into lesser divisions? Any literary work, in order to communicate meaningfully, must have organization. A group of words without structure would be absolutely meaningless. This is not to suggest that there is only *one* way to outline a book. Actually, your outline is your way of retaining the material in the book and recalling it. At this point in your study it is only a *tentative* outline. You will readily learn that some books reveal their structure very quickly, while some are much more difficult to analyze. You are not done with your reading, however, until you have begun to see the book's organization. Naturally, as your study intensifies, you may revise your understanding of some of the details, but the overall pattern should become clear to you at this point. Look for the major divisions, then for subdivisions, then segments that make up these subdivisions, and finally the individual paragraphs that make up these segments. This step of compartmentalization is much more significant than any chapter divisions the published text might include.

(4) *Consider the style.* It is very important to recognize the varying types of literary style and form that you will find in the Scriptures. One does not study poetry exactly the same way as he would prose

narrative; historical biography is not to be considered identical with apocalyptic prophecy. What is the literary form of the material being studied? (Each book may include several different types.) Is there any significance in the fact that the author has used the particular form that he chose?

Perhaps a word is in order concerning the various literary forms that are found in the Scriptures. The first and most common form is *prose narrative*. Here the author is telling a story. The concern of the reader centers upon the characters, events, and locale of the narrative.

A second and frequently used form is that of *discourse*. The author is enlarging upon a theme or an idea in order to instruct his readers. He may record a discourse given by someone else. An excellent illustration of discourse is the Sermon on the Mount found in Matthew 5-7. The reader has the concern of seeing the central idea of the discourse and following its logical argument.

Closely related to the discourse is the *epistle*. Here we have a letter from someone directed either to a church (as in many of the Pauline letters), the Christians in general (as in the so-called General Epistles), or to individuals (for example, Philemon, 1 and 2 Timothy, Titus). The New Testament epistle follows the first century pattern: The author usually identifies himself at the outset, gives his message, and then sends greetings to personal acquaintances. The reader can often learn much about the personal life of the writer as well as follow the argument of the letter.

The book of Job illustrates another form of literature that probably is not clearly found anywhere else, *drama*. The typical ancient drama had a prologue, distinct characters communicating their viewpoint, and an epilogue. It can readily be seen that this is the format by the author of Job. To say this is not to question the *truth* of the story; it is simply to recognize the form in which it is expressed.

There are three types of literature found in the Scriptures that need fuller development than we can give them here. A later chapter will suggest important aids in studying them. The *parable* is a story that parallels a spiritual truth which can clearly be seen if one has the 'key.' *Apocalyptic literature* deals with angelic visitation, visions, symbolic language, etc. (the book of Revelation, the book of Zechariah, portions of Daniel and Ezekiel are apocalyptic in nature). *Poetry* is the third type. It perhaps seems strange that we must have a separate section to deal with poetry, but it is necessary because there are many differences between biblical poetry and the poetic form common to the English language.

(5) *Consider the emotional tone.* Do you sense that the author was angry when he wrote? Joyful? Excited? Worried? Depressed? What do you feel was the emotional reaction of the people to whom he wrote? Would this book cause them to be happy? Resentful? Thankful? These are only suggestive of the varied possibilities that you might discover in reading the material. Be sensitive to the feelings of both author and reader. Then again, it might be helpful to ask yourself, "How does this book make *me* feel? What would be my reaction if it were written to me?" (Remember that in a sense it was written to you!).

(6) *Note significant words and phrases.* It is important to observe what words or terms the author feels are of particular importance. These he will stress in some manner, perhaps by repetition, or

by careful explanation, or by precise definition. You will want to make a note of all such words and phrases, realizing that they will become important clues in explaining the entire picture of the data that makes up the book.

Indeed, we should perhaps pause to underscore the importance of doing all of this work *in writing!* It is amazing how many people think they are reading with an alert mind and absorbing the material and even reacting to it; yet a few days later little remains in their memory. It is of supreme importance that you write down the results as you examine the data. Very often significant insights as to meaning and interpretation come as one restudies the notes that he has taken in the course of his study.

(7) *Additional details to look for.* While you are making yourself thoroughly acquainted with the content of the book that you are studying, there are several other things that should concern you. (a) *Who is the author?* What do you know about him? Was he one of the original apostles or Paul? Does the book specifically mention him as the author? If not, on what do you base your conclusion?

(b) *To whom is he writing?* What can you learn about the city or the church or the individual that received the letter? What special conditions in that city are reflected in the letter?

(c) *When was the book written?* What date can you assign to it? Are there specific references in the body of the book that tie in the work to its historical period?

(d) *Why was the book written?* What was the author's purpose? Does he state it clearly or is it implied? On what do you base your conclusion? Are there particular problems with which the author deals? What are they? Do you feel that he deals with them adequately?

Your immediate reaction might be, "I don't see the answers to all of those questions. How can I find out these details?" Here is where you can receive help from the scholarship that has gone into the study of these books before. You should scrupulously avoid studying commentaries in order to learn what the text means at this point (they will have their place later on), but you can use the introductory, background material to good advantage. The more of this background material with which you are acquainted, the more adequately will you be able to grasp the significant innuendos of the book you are studying.

Let us pause and summarize what we have said up to this point. The very first thing to do when you are seeking to study a book of the Bible is to *read it*—not just once, but as many times as you possibly can. Read it through at one sitting each time, if at all possible. As you progress in the subsequent readings, begin to take notes on the data that you observe. Determine what kind of book it is. Seek to understand it so thoroughly that you can state the major theme of the book in a sentence or two. Try to see the structural design of the book. Remember, any literary work that communicates and makes sense has some structure; the more clearly you can see it, the more effectively you will grasp the meaning of the work. Determine as much as you can about the author, the people to whom he is writing, the purpose that he has in writing, the date when the book was written, and other details that might come through to you in this overall study. You want to seek to recognize literary style and the emotional tone of the work. You will note carefully the words and phrases on which the author seems to put particular stress.

So we come to the conclusion of the first major

step: You have examined the data, endeavoring to see the _whole_ book. Now we are ready to proceed. But first, let's consider some exercises that will help us to put these ideas into practice.

EXERCISES FOR CHAPTER 2

Examining the Data: Seeing the Whole

1. Read the Gospel of John through at one sitting (unit-read); repeat as often as you possibly can.

2. After having unit-read it several times, in what category would you place this book? Would you classify it as biography, history, or what?

3. State the theme of the Gospel of John in one or two sentences.

4. What do you feel is the predominant literary style? Are there examples of other styles?

5. What do you feel are the divisions of this book? What tentative outline do you see?

6. What do you feel you can discern about the author from the book itself? Is there any evidence to indicate to whom he is writing? Do you see anything that would help you to determine the date of the book? What was the author's purpose? Is there anything to help us to understand why he wrote the book?

7. Do some background research concerning the Gospel of John. Check several authorities to determine date, occasion, etc. Remember to avoid their suggestions as to the meaning of the text, but take advantage of their introductory material. (Be sure to record author, title, and page number of your source.)

8. What feelings do you think the author had as he wrote? How do you think his readers felt when they read the book? How does it make *you* feel?

9. What significant words and phrases do you see in this work?

"I could not help laughing at the ease with which he explained his process of deduction. 'When I hear you give your reasons,' I remarked, 'the thing always appears to me to be so ridiculously simple that I could easily do it myself, though at each successive instance of your reasoning I am baffled, until you explain your process. And yet I believe that my eyes are as good as yours.'

" 'Quite so,' he answered, . . . 'You see, but you do not observe. The distinction is clear. For example, you have frequently seen the steps which lead up from the hall to this room.'

" 'Frequently.'

" 'How often?'

" 'Well, some hundreds of times.'

" 'Then how many are there?'

" 'How many! I don't know.'

" 'Quite so! You have not observed. And yet you have seen. That is just my point. Now, I know that there are seventeen steps, because I have both seen and observed.' "

—A Scandal in Bohemia

"I have no data yet. It is a capital mistake to theorize before one has data. Insensibly one begins to twist facts to suit theories instead of theories to suit facts.' "

—A Scandal in Bohemia

"The world is full of obvious things which nobody by any chance ever observes.' "

—The Hound of the Baskervilles

CHAPTER 3

Examining the Data: Organizing the Clues!

The first major step in understanding any written work is to see the whole book, to understand what the entire work is seeking to get across as its message. However, most people are satisfied in getting only a vague impression of the thrust of a book. If you ask them if they have read the particular work, their answer is, "Why, yes, I have read that book." But if you ask them what the author said in the book, or ask them what they remember, all too often their response indicates they did not absorb anything of the book's message.

Part of the difficulty is that we often read *passively*. We get ourselves into a comfortable position and *read pages*. (Often school assignments foster this kind of thing; the professor asks the class to "read pages 26-45 for the next class session," and the student dutifully reads the pages but does not actually think of what the author is saying.) We must learn to read *actively*. Look at the book as a direct communication to you. Learn to react to each statement; talk back if necessary. Others may think you are a bit foolish to talk to a book, but if it will help you to really grasp its message, what of it? Get your mind really involved in what is being said.

When we have accomplished the reading and re-reading of the book, we have only just begun. Now we are ready to come to grips with what the author is seeking to tell us. We suggested earlier that one might take the analogy of a detective seeking to solve a crime. The first thing he must do is to take in the entire scene of the crime. Everyone is urged to leave things exactly as they were until the trained mind can *examine the data as a whole.* But then the work of the detective is only starting. He must carefully scrutinize every detail that he can find: a scrap of hair, a torn button, a smudge of grease, a telltale fingerprint, a broken glass—these are the things out of which he reconstructs what probably took place.

The clues with which we concern ourselves in studying the Word of God are, perhaps obviously, the *words* that are used. We must turn to the first paragraph of the first segment and begin to apply ourselves to an understanding of the words. It is not enough that we know what the words *mean* in terms of a dictionary definition. We must determine what *this* author means by the word in this sentence.

Consider carefully the following hypothetical exchange between a professor and his students:

"What does the word 'train' mean?"

" 'A series of railroad cars in sequence.' "

"I see. Then I can understand the society note, 'The bride came down the aisle followed by her series of railroad cars in sequence'!"

"Oh, no! That would be a long veil."

"Oh, so 'train' means 'long veil'! I noticed that Mayor Lindsay was walking the streets of Harlem the other day with a large number of reporters in his long veil!"

"No, no! There the word means 'followers in a company.' "

"Oh, all right. 'Train' means 'followers in a company.' Last week the soccer coach told the team that they were expected to follow in a company in order to be ready and in shape for the next season."

"No, no! There the word is a verb and it means 'to bring into desired physical shape by means of diet and exercise.' "

"Then you really don't know what the word 'train' means?"

"Not until you use it in a sentence!"

Exactly right! You do not know what an author means by a word until he uses it in a sentence. The fact of the matter is that often a word can have multiple meanings, even though there is usually a unifying factor present in each of them. The word 'train,' for example, has the varied meanings mentioned, yet there is a thread of commonality. The root idea is "following along in a sequence"; but the specific idea must be learned in the context.

In order to distinguish these varied uses of a single word, we often refer to them as 'terms.' A term might be defined as "a given word in a given context with a specific meaning." Mr. Adler, in his work previously cited, has a chapter entitled "Coming to Terms," in which he says that we must "find the important words and through them come to terms with the author." [1] That is, we must discover what the author means by the word he uses.

Perhaps you are wondering about the relevance of this entire matter to Bible study. After all, does not everyone know what the words mean when he reads a passage? This question can be convincingly answered by considering a number of scripture passages, such as <u>Isaiah 6:1</u>, "In the year that king Uzziah died I saw also the Lord sitting upon a throne, high and lifted up, and his *train* filled the temple." Now, what is the meaning of the word 'train'? Did Isaiah mean "a long veil," perhaps of light or glory? Obviously he did not mean "a series of railroad cars"! Did he mean "followers in his company"? You must seek by every means possible to determine what Isaiah meant by the words that he used.

1. Identify and Define the Terms

Now we are ready for the first step in the second phase of our work: Identify and define the important terms which the author uses. We turn to the first paragraph of the first segment of whatever book we are studying and we carefully scrutinize the clues, that is, the words, to determine what are the important terms of the author. Immediately, the beginning student is faced with a perplexing problem: "<u>How can I know what terms are important?</u>" Let us consider some simple ways to identify them.

<u>First</u>, reread the paragraph, making every effort to understand what the author is saying. Now, are there *any words that you do not understand*? Obviously, if a word is unfamiliar to you, it becomes an important word in the present instance, because you cannot grasp the passage if you do not recognize the words that serve as its building blocks. One thing to keep in mind here is that different readers will differ at this point. A word that is unfamiliar to you may be perfectly clear to someone else. But you must be concerned with the words unfamiliar to you, because this is *your* work!

<u>Secondly</u>, identify the terms that are *central* to the

message. These are the terms that communicate the basic ideas of the sentence or paragraph. If you were to eliminate them, the entire idea would be altered or lost.

Thirdly, take note of any words that have a *deep and profound meaning*. There are certain terms that are always important, simply because the ideas which they communicate are so significant. For example, the terms love, grace, sin, salvation, mercy, peace, etc., would never be overlooked as insignificant in a specific passage.

Then, in your quest for important words, record those terms upon which the *author places particular stress*. Does he go to lengths to define what he means by a certain term? Does he underline it, or set it off in *italics*? Perhaps you will detect that he is arguing about what he means by the word in contrast to what others seem to mean by it. A good instance of this can be seen in the discussion in James 2:14-26. The author is concerned because he feels strongly that many believers in his day simply have misunderstood the meaning of faith. Apparently, there were those who thought that faith was simply an intellectual assent to certain doctrines unrelated to life. James vehemently asserts that faith must affect behavior or it is not true faith. Certainly anyone can see that the term 'faith' is important in this paragraph because the author puts up such a strong argument about it.

Now as to procedure—you should not only note these clues in your mind, you must record them on paper. Record each significant term and seek to define it as you feel the author is using it. This will be a tentative judgment while you continue to study the passage; you cannot be sure of the meaning that the author has in mind until you examine the structure of the passage and see clearly how the term is used.

But *defining* the term is not sufficient in itself. One must also determine if the author is using it *literally* or *figuratively*. A term is literal if it is used in its basic stated sense according to its definition. For example, if an author uses the term *tree*, the literal sense would refer to a large woody plant consisting of trunk, branches, leaves and a root system. But we use the term in many other ways:

1. When he was chased by the bear he climbed a *tree*.

2. The students asked so many questions that he soon was up a *tree*.

3. Miss Prim delighted in searching out her family *tree*.

4. Mr. Brown sought to improve the landscaping of his property by planting a *tree* in the yard.

5. The Scriptures say that the righteous man is like a *tree* planted by the rivers of water.

6. Just inside the door you will find a clothes *tree*.

It can readily be noted that in statements 1 and 4 the term 'tree' is being used in its literal sense. In the other statements reference is not made to an actual woody plant. Figurative language is based upon the principle of *analogy*. There is some characteristic of a tree that enables us to use the figure to make our language more vivid. So in 2 we use the expression "up a tree" to indicate someone who is confined in his direction; he is in a position from which there is no retreat. In 3 the expression "family tree" uses the analogy of the many branches developing from a single seed to apply to the children of a common ancestor. The "clothes tree" in 6 uses the analogy of the branches of a tree as applied to the portions of the wooden upright piece of furniture that provides 'branches' upon which to hang clothes.

In statement 5 we have a special use of figurative language, the figure of speech. Since we will deal with the chief figures of speech in common use in English in our section on literary structure, we will not enlarge upon it here. Note that, taken by itself, 'tree' might seem to be literal here (i.e., "planted by rivers of water"), but in the completed structure we see the comparison being made between a man and a tree.

Is it really important to identify figurative language? Most definitely! If you fail to see the term as figurative, you will also fail to see the analogy that the author is making, and therefore you will fail to understand his message. Jesus said, "I am the door: by me if any man enter in, he shall be saved" (John 10:9). We must see that He is saying that just as there is a proper access into the sheepfold literally, so He is the only access into salvation.

② Study the Paragraph Structure

That brings us to our next step: Take careful note of the grammatical and literary structure of the paragraph. Actually, we are seeking to clearly see how the terms are interrelated; how they are built together (hence, structure). In its outworking this step is concerned with three parts. Perhaps it will help to deal with them separately.

✳ Grammatical Structure

There are few subjects that most students dislike more intensely than grammar.* They come out

---

* It is understood that knowledge of the original language can

of secondary schools every year, unable to parse a simple sentence (or indeed, to even define what it means to parse a sentence!), and with an emotional aversion to the entire subject. Nonetheless, if you are going to understand written material, you must be able to see and comprehend the grammatical interrelationships of the phrases and sentences. You have already defined the meaning of the verbal idea in the sentence, and the meaning of the nouns, pronouns, adjectives, etc., that make up the remaining part of the sentence. (In defining them you should have sought to clarify for yourself what part of speech the given term has in the sentence.) Now the important thing is to see the relationships between these terms.

Suppose we begin with the verbal idea. We will assume that in noticing the significant words and phrases, you have already determined the meaning of the verb. It is not enough just to know what the word means. What *tense* does the author use in expressing the verb? Does he suggest that the action took place in the past, that it is taking place in the present, or that it will take place in the future? Furthermore, what is the *mood* of the verb?

Perhaps it might be a good idea to review what the possible moods are. First, a verb may be in the *indicative* mood. The author here is indicating definite action. He is suggesting that the action is actual. It either *did* take place (past tense), or it *is* taking

---

be of great help in detailed study. Since this work is concerned with methodology for studying the English Bible, we will confine ourselves to English grammatical rules. In the following section only the basic patterns are discussed. The more thoroughly the student masters the intricacies of English grammar, the more thorough will be his study of the Word of God.

place (present tense), or it *will* take place (future tense).

On the other hand, it is possible that the author wishes to suggest action that is possible or perhaps probable. Here he would use the *subjunctive* mood. The action *may have* taken place (past tense), *may be* taking place (present tense), or *may* take place (future tense). Since the subjunctive is the mood of *potential* action, it has a future time idea. If it had already happened, it would move out of potential action to definite action and would no longer be subjunctive.

The third major mood presents the action in terms of a command. This is the *imperative* mood. Just as the indicative presents action that is definitely true, and the subjunctive presents action that is potentially true, so the imperative presents action that is volitionally true. That is, if the recipient of the command chooses to obey, the action will be realized.

Once we have established the tense and mood of the verb, we still need to be certain that we understand the *voice*. Here we are concerned with the question, "What is the relationship between the subject and the action?" If the subject is performing the action, the verb is in the *active* voice (e.g., "The boy *hit* the ball"). On the other hand, if the subject is receiving the action, we are confronted with the *passive* voice (e.g., "The boy *was hit* by the ball").

Now that we have analyzed the verb, we are ready to notice the other relationships. It is helpful to start with the main verb of the paragraph and then ask yourself, "What is the *subject* of this verb? the *direct object*? the *indirect object*?" All other dependent clauses, phrases, etc., cluster around one of these four main parts.

To look at it another way, there are four main parts to every sentence or independent clause: (1) subject, (2) verb, (3) direct object, (4) indirect object. This is not to suggest that all four must *always* be present, but rather to emphasize that everything else in the sentence will be subordinate to one of these four.

In dealing, then, with a difficult sentence or paragraph, it might be helpful to write the main parts of the statement in BOLD TYPE vertically, showing how the rest of the parts relate to them.[2] For example, suppose you are studying John 6:51; your work sheet might look like this:

JOHN 6:51

	I (subject)
	AM (verb)
the living	BREAD (predicate nominative with verb of being—takes place of direct object)
	which came down from heaven:
(Conditional clause)	if any man eat of this bread, he shall live forever:
	and (conjunction)
the	BREAD that I will give
	IS
my	FLESH, which I will give for the life of the world.

The student can readily see a number of advantages to this. There is a clarity of understanding that comes through. Note how this simple device clears up the confusion expressed by the Jews in verse 52. When you see the relationship between the two main thoughts, it is clear that we are dealing with figurative analogy. Just as Jesus is not literally bread, so His flesh is not literally bread. We are to understand that He is to be the main sustenance of our spiritual lives as bread is the main sustenance of our physical lives.

Let us turn to another illustration. Some of Paul's sentences are rather involved, but they can be clarified by this method. Examine how you might structure Ephesians 1:15-19.

EPHESIANS 1:15-19

Wherefore (connective)
I (subject) also,

and
after I heard of your
—faith in the Lord Jesus,
—love unto all the saints,

CEASE NOT (verb)
TO GIVE THANKS (infinitive used as direct object)
FOR YOU (indirect object), making mention of you in my prayers;
That (conjunction)
the GOD of our Lord Jesus Christ, the Father of glory,
MAY GIVE (verb in subjunctive mood)
UNTO YOU (indirect object)
the SPIRIT (direct object) of wisdom and revelation in the knowledge of him:

The eyes of your understanding being enlightened;

that (conjunction, "in order that")
YE
MAY KNOW
WHAT is the hope of his calling,

| (3-fold direct object) | and | WHAT the riches of the glory of his inheritance in the saints, |
| | and | WHAT is the exceeding greatness of his power to us-ward who believe. |

(The remainder of chapter 1, verses 19b-23, is a further development of "the greatness of his power.")

Note how this technique enables you to sort out the dependent clauses and to see that Paul is describing his two-sided prayer for the Ephesians, both of thanksgiving for their faith and love and of request for their increased knowledge.

It is not to be supposed that this practice needs to be followed for every sentence. Where the student clearly sees the structure and readily discerns the main parts of the sentence, it may not be necessary. However, whether or not one diagrams a sentence, he must see the relationship of every phrase and clause to the main parts of the sentence.

The student who is weak in his knowledge of English grammar would do well to secure a summary review of the basic principles so that he can recognize dependent and independent clauses, various types of phrases, etc.

Literary Structure

We turn now to the second major feature of structure: the *literary techniques* that the author uses. These are not to be confused with literary form, or style, such as we discussed earlier (prose, poetry, etc.). Here we are concerned with various methods that the writer uses to capture attention and to express his thoughts with vividness. We will discuss ten of these techniques with the hope that the student will seek to develop an awareness of them so as to recognize their use. In addition, we will discuss some of the most common figures of speech that are used to convey ideas with greater forcefulness and dynamic.

The following literary techniques are given roughly in the order of common usage in literature. It is to be understood, however, that all of them are very widely used. It should also be pointed out that this list is more suggestive than exhaustive. There are other techniques with which the serious student may wish to become familiar.

(1) *Comparison*: In seeking to express his thoughts clearly and vividly, any author frequently resorts to comparing the unknown, which he seeks to communicate, with the known that is understood by his readers. One can almost sense the author saying to himself, "Let me see, how can I describe this? What comparison can I make? What is it like?" The result is an analogy of some sort, either using figurative language, as described earlier, or using one of the many available figures of speech (described below). When the author writes, "Though your sins be as scarlet, they shall be as white as snow; though they be red like crimson, they shall be as wool" (Isa. 1:18), one can safely assume that his readers know something about snow and wool, and that the connotation of scarlet and crimson adds to the seriousness of the situation. They may not understand too much about sins, but the comparison will aid their knowledge.

(2) *Contrast*: Often the concern of the author is best expressed by contrast rather than comparison. While in comparison you are showing how two things are the same, in contrast you are showing how they differ. Note the effective use of contrast in Psalm 1 where the psalmist describes the blessing of the man who loves the law of the Lord and then says,

"The ungodly are not so: but are like the chaff." The contrast between a planted tree and windblown chaff is just about as absolute as one can state.

(3) *Repetition*: An effective way to underscore the importance of something is to state it over and over again. This may be done by the constant re-echoing of the same words, as in Psalm 136 when the poet expresses the beautiful refrain, "His mercy endureth forever," in every verse. Or again the writer may repeat the same idea, using different words.

(4) *Summarization*: Often an author will seek to clarify his thoughts by gathering together the main ideas that he has been seeking to express, and then restating them in summary. Note how the writer to the Hebrews begins the eighth chapter: "Now of the things which we have spoken this is the sum." He then proceeds to gather together the chief thoughts and to express them again.

(5) *Explanation*: If the author senses that he is using terms or expressing ideas that are not clear to his readers, he may seek to take time to explain them to his readers. Note how Luke describes the incident when Joseph and Mary bring Jesus to Jerusalem as a Babe "to present him to the Lord." Fearing that his readers may not understand the meaning, he quotes from Exodus 13:2 to explain their action (Luke 2:22, 23).

(6) *Interrogation*: The technique of anticipating a question and then proceeding to answer it is a technique often used by the apostle Paul. As you study the book of Romans this will be evident to you. In Romans 3:1 he writes, "What advantage then hath the Jew? or what profit is there of circumcision?" And again in 6:1, "What shall we say then? Shall we continue in sin, that grace may abound?" As he proceeds to answer the questions, he presents profound truth.

Interrogation is also used in prose narrative where the writer records a conversation between two or more participants involving questions and answers. Note this in John 3 and in many other incidents in the gospel story.

(7) *Climax:* A very important technique which almost any author uses is that of building his material up to a point of climax. In the gospel story, Jesus seems to be vitally concerned first with instructing His intimate disciples concerning himself until they come to the conviction expressed in Matthew 16:16, "Thou art the Christ, the Son of the living God." Only then can He proceed to tell them of His approaching death. This then is a climax to His early ministry, just as the open tomb is the climax to His passion. In order to see the climax in a passage, the student must concern himself with relationships and interrelationships between the paragraphs and sections of the book.

Sometimes the author is quite explicit in expressing climax. Note this in John 12:23-36 where John records Jesus' final revelation of himself to the people and then His withdrawal. It is obvious that when He hid himself from them, His ministry to the people was over.

(8) *Causation:* Often an author will seek to explain the reason for the existence of a certain situation. He may attempt to describe it from the standpoint of moving from cause to effect, as in Galatians 6:7, "Do not be deceived; God is not mocked, for whatever a man sows, that he will also reap." Here the apostle makes clear that the cause of one's sowing leads to inevitable results. Whenever an author makes a prediction of the results of certain behavior, he is using causation.

Occasionally this might be done from the opposite direction. The author might look at the evidence and move backward from the effect to the cause. Notice Paul's statement to the Athenians in Acts 17:22, "I perceive that in every way you are very religious. For as I passed along, and observed the objects of your worship, I found also an altar with this inscription, 'To an unknown God.' " Here Paul describes what he sees, and draws a conclusion as to what had caused it.

(9) *Generalization:* Here is a useful technique that an author or speaker can use. He makes a series of observations and leads up to a conclusion or principle based upon them. Note in Romans 8 how Paul builds up the evidence of the wonderful activity of the Holy Spirit in our behalf, and then concludes with the principle in verse 31, "What then shall we say to this? If God is for us, who is against us?"

(10) *Particularization:* The author may choose to use the opposite technique from generalization. That is, he may elect to make an inclusive statement, then present details to support it. An excellent example of this is in Matthew 6. The Lord Jesus makes the general statement in verse 1, "Beware of practicing your piety before men in order to be seen by them." He then proceeds to illustrate what He means in the next four paragraphs as applied to almsgiving, praying and fasting.

It is not to be supposed that these are the only literary techniques one will note. They are among the most important and the most frequently used.

One further area needs to be examined as we consider the matter of literary structure. Very often, in seeking especially to demonstrate comparison or contrast, the author will resort to what we call *figures of speech*. These must be carefully noted so that the main truth that is being presented might be clearly grasped. Some of the more common figures of speech are presented here,[4] and the student is urged to be on the alert to recognize examples from the Scriptures.

(1) *Simile* (from the Latin *similis*, "like" or "similar"): In this very common figure of speech the author compares two or more entities, using the comparative adverbs, 'like,' 'as,' or 'so.' Examples abound throughout the Scriptures (and indeed in all literature). The prophet cries out, "All we *like* sheep have gone astray" (Isa. 53:6). In Matthew 13 Jesus gives a series of parables prefaced by the statement, "The kingdom of heaven is *like*" (Matt. 13:44ff.).

(2) *Metaphor* (from the Greek *meta,* "over," and *pherein,* "to bear"): Even more commonly used in the Scriptures than the simile, the metaphor is a forceful implied comparison without the use of the adverb. Some characteristic of one thing is "carried over" and applied to another. It is a stronger figure than a simile. Note, for example, how much more forceful is Jesus' statement, "I am the bread of life," than the simile counterpart, "I am like bread."

(3) *Personification:* This is a figure of speech in which inanimate things are given characteristics of life, and impersonal things are given personality. Note Jesus' statement in response to the Jewish leaders who asked Him to rebuke the disciples for their messianic outbursts, "I tell you, if these were silent, the very stones would cry out" (Luke 19:40).

(4) *Anthropomorphism* (from the Greek *anthropos,* "man," and *morphe,* "form"): Frequently the writers of the Scriptures speak of God as having human form. With the exception of the incarnation of the Lord Jesus, and those preincarnate appearances of the Lord in human form (as in Genesis 18), these references constitute figures of speech. God is a Spirit and does not have a body. Consider

the statement of the prophets, "The hand of the Lord was there upon him" (Ezek. 1:3; compare Jer. 1:9). The psalmist speaks of God "whose eyes keep watch on the nations" (Ps. 66:7).

(5) *Analogy* (from the Greek *ana*, "according to," and *logos*, "proportion"): The analogy is not always referred to as a figure of speech because it is often fuller than a simple statement. (In this regard it is similar to an allegory, which is an extended metaphor, often in story form.) In the analogy the writer expresses comparison by showing how the characteristics of one situation are paralleled in another setting of quite different circumstances. For example, in Psalm 23 the poet begins with a metaphor, "The Lord is my shepherd." But the next portion of the psalm, verses 2-4, compares the relationship of a shepherd to his sheep, and the Lord to His own. Failure to recognize the analogy leads to confusion. For example, in verses 5 and 6 the analogy changes to that of the relationship between a host and his guest. If one fails to note the change, much of the impact of the psalm can be lost.

In addition to these figures of speech that are primarily concerned with comparisons of one kind or another, there are several types which have to do with the method of expression, enabling the thought of the writer to come through with greater vividness.

(6) *Irony* (from the Greek *eiron*, "a dissembler in speech"): This is a technique whereby the writer, in either humor or sarcasm, states something directly opposite to what he actually means. Note the strong impact of Paul's ironic passage in 1 Corinthians 4:8-13, especially verse 10, "We are fools for Christ's sake, but you are wise in Christ. We are weak, but you are strong. You are held in honor, but we in disrepute."

(7) *Hyperbole* (from the Greek *hyper*, "over," and *ballein*, "to throw"—an "overshooting, excess"): Here the writer uses a planned exaggeration to convey his point. He emphasizes a fact by overstatement. Jesus said, "It is easier for a camel to go through the eye of a needle, than for a rich man to enter into the kingdom of God" (Mark 10:25). Many strange interpretations have developed over this passage because of failing to see the hyperbole that the Master was using. He was not teaching the difficulty of salvation by human effort; He was teaching its impossibility!

(8) *Paradox* (from the Greek *para*, "beyond," and *doxon*, "opinion," from *dokein*, "to think, suppose"): This is a strong expression which at first hearing seems to involve an absurdity or even a contradiction. But as one meditates on the statement, the forcefulness of the truth is communicated. Mark quotes Jesus as saying, "Whoever would save his life will lose it; and whoever loses his life for my sake and the gospel's will save it" (8:35). Was there ever a more forceful reminder to put first things first?

Two further figures of speech should be discussed. They have to do with flexibility of expression.

(9) *Synecdoche* (from the Greek *synekdechesthai*, "to receive together with"): Here the author uses a part for the whole, or the whole for a part. We understand his meaning from the context, and the figure makes the significance more vivid. When John the Baptist was confronted by the religious leaders and asked to identify himself, his reply was, "I am the voice of one crying in the wilderness, 'Make straight the way of the Lord'" (John 1:23). Here the word 'voice' is used as representative of the prophetic spokesman whom Isaiah had promised. Paul, in one of those pathetic final statements in

2 Timothy, states to his "son in the faith," "You are aware that all who are in Asia turned away from me" (1:15). It is obvious that we are not to conclude that Paul had not one friend left in the entire province, but the figure makes his disappointment ring with greater poignancy.

(10) *Metonymy* (from the Greek *meta*, suggesting "change," and *onoma*, "a name"): Here a writer may substitute one word for another, particularly giving the cause for the effect, or the effect for the cause. It is also used when one substitutes the container for the thing contained. Jesus cried out, "Shall I not drink the cup which the Father has given me?" (John 18:11). An illustration of substituting a cause for an effect is in Job 34:6, "My *arrow* is incurable." Here he obviously is referring to the wound caused by an arrow.

It is not to be supposed that this list exhausts the potential figures of speech that one might find. The serious student would be profited by an effort to discover the meaning and use of the *oxymoron,* the *paronomasia,* the *anthropopathy,* the *litotes,* the *zeugma,* and others. Nonetheless, a careful recognition of these ten will be of great profit to the student.

Paragraph Structure

We have seen how that the student must be a careful observer of the terms of the passage and also of how those terms are put together from both a grammatical and literary perspective. There is yet a third aspect of structure with which we must concern ourselves: the structure of each paragraph.

Once you have noted the terms and the grammatical and literary structure that relates them, it is important that you take each paragraph and determine what the focus and thrust of the paragraph is. When you first began to study literature, you were taught to identify the topic sentence, the one that expresses the chief idea of that paragraph; the other sentences contribute to the idea by supplying background, effect, description or implications.

Once you have isolated the chief idea, it is well to give the paragraph a temporary study title. This title will enable you to have a handle with which to maneuver the particular paragraph as you seek to integrate it into the larger segment.

It should be noted that this is a *temporary* title. Don't confuse this with your final summary title, which will be discussed later. You may find yourself changing this title several times as you work with the relationships between paragraphs.

Having seen the central thought of the paragraph, you should next seek to group the paragraph with the others that deal with the same general subject. In theory at least, as you examined the book from the whole to the parts, you should have seen the major divisions and some of the subdivisions. Now you are moving in the opposite direction: grouping *paragraphs* into *segments*, segments into *subdivisions*, and subdivisions into the major *divisions* of the book.

Let us illustrate by turning to the Gospel of John. You have unit-read the Gospel and made a conscious effort to see its parts. Now you are working back from the parts to the whole. There is a close relationship between the eight paragraphs of chapter 1. Yet, as one studies the individual paragraphs, one becomes aware that the first four paragraphs should be grouped together. They are all discussing the "Word-Light" who became flesh. The last four paragraphs, on the other hand, are concerned with the ministry of John the Baptist and the steady surrender of the focus of attention from John to Jesus.

As you study the paragraph structure, you discover the main theme of each given paragraph, and then you group paragraphs into segments. Here again it might be helpful to give a tentative title to each segment. Paragraphs 5-8 of John 1 might be called "John Introduces Jesus."

Your entire concern up to this point has been to see what is there. You have been *examining the data.* Perhaps you have concluded that that's all there is to it. But we are just beginning. Before moving on, however, a word is in order about procedure.

It is absolutely imperative that you learn to *record what you see.* As you examine the clues, you must write down what you see. In a carefully numbered sequence record each detail that you observe. There are several things to avoid:

(1) Don't simply write down a quotation. This is not necessary, as you have it in your text. If you are simply quoting, you are not really *seeing.* What is there about that quotation that makes you feel that it is important? Get behind the words to the *idea.* For example, if you record, "In the beginning was the Word," as an observation of John 1:1, you are kidding yourself. You have some vague feeling that this is important. But what is it saying? Should not the observation be something like this: "Something identified only as 'the Word' is described as existing already when everything began"?

(2) Don't simply paraphrase the text. If you are just saying the same thing in other words, all of the objections to quoting still apply.

(3) Don't just summarize the statement. Again you are not *seeing* what is there. This is very similar to quoting or paraphrasing.

(4) Don't simply write down a word. What is significant about it? What is its relation to the sentence? It is well always to express your observations in complete sentences. This forces you to express why you think what you have seen is important.

(5) Don't simply give an outline of the paragraph. You are again not grappling with what the author is saying.

(6) Your paragraph title is not an observation. It is a convenient working device. It grows out of your observations.

(7) Be certain that you are recording what you *see*, not what you have heard about the passage, or what someone has told you. Often when students study Mark they will record as an observation, "This Gospel was written to Romans," hardly an observation of the text.

"But," you may be asking yourself, "if none of these things are really observations, what *is* a genuine observation?" Let us look at a brief passage to illustrate how you might record your observations. Suppose you were studying Psalm 1. You have carefully and thoroughly read it a number of times and have concluded that it is a poetic statement of the differences between the righteous man and the ungodly man. Now you are ready to observe and record what you see. Perhaps your paper would look something like this:

1. The psalmist states that a certain person who evidences certain characteristics is in a state described by the predicate adverb "blessed."

2. The definite article "the" is used to modify this man.

3. The verb "is" is in the present tense. We are not told that this man *will be* blessed, but that he "is" blessed.

4. The man is described by a threefold series of negative dependent clauses. Each of these clauses reveals a progression of physical position: walking, standing, sitting.

5. Each of the verbs in these progressive clauses is in the present tense.

6. The negative verb "not walking" is modified by the prepositional phrase "in the counsel [advice] of the ungodly." The blessed man's walk does not follow the advice that issues from ungodly people.

7. The negative verb "nor standing" is modified by the prepositional phrase "in the way of sinners." The blessed man does not find himself standing in the path or concourse habituated by sinful people.

8. The negative verb "nor sitting" is modified by the prepositional phrase "in the seat of the scornful." The blessed man does not sit down in the company of those who are sneering at spiritual things.

9. There seems to be a significance in the progression of these three clauses, as though one would lead to the other, etc.

10. The second sentence (v. 2) begins with the adversative "but," indicating a reversal of thought, here turning from what this man in question does *not* do, to what he *does* do.

11. One must also observe that the poet has chosen to express the negative (what he does *not* do) before the positive (what he *does* do).

Please do not assume that these eleven observations exhaust the material in verse 1. They are simply illustrative. Perhaps this will suffice to demonstrate what you should be doing at this point. This is the *heart* of personal Bible study. In some respects it is the hardest work of all. We must discipline ourselves to see *everything* that will help us in understanding the passage. The more we *see*, the more we have to work with in coming to a thorough understanding of the passage.

The good student always works with pen in hand, prepared to record the results of his work. Develop your own best method to record the things that you see, but be certain to record them. There is nothing more common than the experience of the student who sees something with real insight and is so blessed that he thinks, "I'll never forget that," only to lose it the next day because it was not recorded.

There is one final thing to take note of in the passage that you are studying. This has to do with *proportion*. How much comparative space does the author give to a particular subject? We reason that if he spends a good deal of time developing a particular theme, it must be important to him.

When you carefully study the Gospel accounts, you notice that a large portion of each Gospel deals with the last week of our Lord's ministry. The Triumphal Entry occurred on Palm Sunday, five days before the Crucifixion. This event is recorded in Matthew 21, Mark 11, Luke 19, and John 12. Matthew devotes 8 chapters out of 28 (28%), Mark 6 chapters out of 16 (37 1/2%), Luke 6 chapters out of 24 (25%), and John 10 chapters out of 21 (48%), to the events of this last week. Surely we can see that the Holy Spirit desires us to grasp the importance of this last week.

Not only do we need to see the things to which the author devotes the greatest space; we must also see the contrast between what he says and what he does not say. Everything in the Word of God is important; it has been selected from the total of what could be said in order to accomplish the purpose of the Holy Spirit. John concludes his Gospel account with the suggestion that if everything that the Lord did and said were recorded, the whole world would not be able to contain the books (John 21:24). We must then realize that the things that are recorded are important for us to know and understand.

We see, then, that the second step in our personal Bible study is to examine the data, looking at each of the clues that will help our understanding. Let us consider a few exercises in order to help us in this part of our study.

EXERCISES FOR CHAPTER 3

Examining the Data: Organizing the Clues!

1. Carefully examine the eight paragraphs of chapter 1 of John. Note and record everything that you see that you consider significant. Include the important terms; the significant relationships between terms, both grammatical and literary; the relationships between the paragraphs; the proportion of truth in the segment.

2. Specifically identify the literary techniques and the figures of speech that you observe in this unit.

3. Seek to give a working title to each paragraph that seems to you to capture the main idea of the paragraph. Also give a title to those groups of paragraphs that seem to belong together.

"Let me indicate a possible line of thought. It is, I admit, mere imagination, but how often is imagination the mother of truth?"

—The Valley of Fear

"Breadth of view, my dear Mr. Mac, is one of the essentials of our profession. The interplay of ideas and the oblique uses of knowledge are often of extraordinary in-interest."

—The Valley of Fear

" 'But was it not mere guesswork?'
" 'No, No; I never guess. It is a shocking habit—destructive to the logical faculty. What seems strange to you is only so because you do not follow my train of thought or observe the small facts upon which large inference may depend.' "

—The Sign of the Four

"The more outré and grotesque an incident is the more carefully it deserves to be examined, and the very point which appears to complicate a case is, when duly considered and scientifically handled, the one which is most likely to elucidate it."

—The Hound of the Baskervilles

CHAPTER 4

Questioning the Data

Up to this point our concern has been with the basic task of *seeing what is there*. Despite the apparent simplicity of what we have been saying, it might be well to underscore the fact that our greatest difficulty in studying any material is in the area of observation. We simply do not discipline ourselves to see the data clearly and in proper perspective.

The next step in studying inductively is to raise questions about what we see. All true learning comes as a result of personal involvement, and we become involved to the degree in which we raise questions. Every professor knows the experience of presenting an exceptionally important unit of his subject and pausing to ask, "Are there any questions?" and getting no response. He knows that either the material has been presented so clearly that every student understands it perfectly, or, much more likely, the students are so confused that they don't know how to ask questions.

Actually there are psychological factors that tend to prevent us from asking questions. Our human pride seeks to keep us from admitting we do not understand. Often we fail to grasp the simple fact that if we do not see the thing clearly, probably many others of our classmates do not see it either.

Jesus, on more than one occasion, told us that we must become as little children in order to enter the kingdom of heaven.[1] One cannot help but wonder if at least one of the things He had in mind was the child's eagerness to learn by asking questions. Many a parent has been driven to the point of exasperation by the persistent questioning of his child. The late comedienne, Miss Fanny Brice, made her fortune by popularizing this feature of childhood with her characterization of Baby Snooks on the radio. Her familiar "Why, Daddy?" is clearly etched on the memory of anyone who lived in the 1940's.

One evening the writer was walking out under the stars with his little six-year-old daughter. The night was clear and crisp and the twinkling heavenly host seemed particularly brilliant. We walked thoughtfully, hand in hand, when suddenly she asked, "Daddy, why don't the stars fall down?" This was no time for a lecture on the intergravitational pull of the heavenly bodies upon one another, yet it was an ideal time for learning. The question had come from the depths of her own being. She had seen everything else that was thrown into the air fall back to earth; she had observed apples fall from their tree. I chose to use that moment for some spiritual instruction as I replied, "Honey, the stars stay in the sky because Jesus keeps them there!" —and so He does. Paul wrote to the Colossian church, "And in him [Jesus] all things hold together" (Col. 1:17).

It was Huxley who was reputed to have said, "I sat down before the facts as a little child." Why as a little child? In order to question what he saw! We may not agree with many of his conclusions, but we cannot find fault with his method.

Let us return briefly to our analogy of the detective. After he has examined the scene of the crime and gathered the clues that he finds there, what is his next step? He begins to ask questions. Any detective story fan is familiar with the line, "I'm Detective So-and-So; I would like to ask you a few questions."

The purpose of the questioning is to enable the skilled detective to see the relationship between each of the clues, and to seek to reconstruct the events as they actually took place.

What are some of the questions that the reader might ask as he seeks to understand the text? It was the English writer, Rudyard Kipling, who gave us a little four-line quotation that might well be committed to memory as a guide:

I have six faithful serving men
Who taught me all I know.
Their names are *What* and *Where* and *When*
And *How* and *Why* and *Who.*[2]

It will readily be seen that three of these questions deal with specific data in the paragraph and will not necessarily be pertinent to every paragraph. The question *where* concerns itself with any locational material. Does the incident occur indoors or outdoors? Is there a specific geographical location given? In what province or city does the action take place?

In much the same way the question *when* seeks to enable the reader to pinpoint any temporal references that may be in the paragraph. This temporal datum might show the relationship between the present paragraph and that which precedes. For example, the phrase "After these things" shows sequential time. On the other hand, the time of day might be given, or the day of the week, or the year might be identified.

In this regard it is well to keep in mind that one must understand the pattern of reckoning time in first-century Judea. The years were related to the reigning emperor. So Jesus was born "in the fifteenth year of the reign of Tiberius Caesar." [3] The day began (for the Jews) at sunset, and was made up of three watches of varying lengths as the days grew longer or shorter. The hours of the day would begin at sunrise (approximately 6:00 a.m.) and be numbered first, second, third, etc., until sunset. In the New Testament, the Roman method of dividing the night into four watches is sometimes reflected, although the old method of three watches probably persisted as well. [4]

The third of our specific questions seeks to help us to distinguish the persons who are involved in the passage. We ask the question *who* so as to see clearly those individuals who are involved in the action or message of the passage. Failure to ask this question can lead to serious misinterpretation. One of the most common illustrations has to do with the familiar statement of Paul in Romans 8:28. We so often hear this quoted, "All things work together for good." But the careful student studying the passage must ask, "*Who* is involved in this verse?" and he sees very clearly that this promise is applicable only to "those who love God, to those who are called according to His purpose." [5]

Perhaps another illustration is in order. Across many public libraries in this country one sees the engraved verse, "The Truth Shall Make You Free."

Now let's examine that verse. What Jesus actually said was, "If you abide in My word, then you are truly disciples of Mine; and you shall know the truth, and the truth shall make you free." [6] The student of the Word, in asking the question *who*, discovers that this only applies to those who believe in the Lord! In other words, it is not education and knowledge that frees; it is faith in the Lord Jesus that makes knowledge of the truth possible!

The fourth question is also somewhat limited because it has to do with methodology. The question is *how*, and again it does not apply to every paragraph. Nonetheless the thoughtful student is alert to the potential in the question. Jesus heals a blind man. Observing this the student asks, "*How* did He do it?" It is fascinating to observe that Jesus used many different methods of healing blind men. He did not want us to focus our attention on the *method* but on the *Master.*

Perhaps the passage under study is discursive in type. We must still be ready to ask how. Note how Nicodemus responded when Jesus spoke to him of the new birth, "*How* can these things be?" Surely this is a question we must all ask and to which we must find the answer.

Four of our questions, then, are concerned with details. We must be alert to them always, but we recognize that not every paragraph will have temporal (*when?*), local (*where?*), modal (*how?*), or identifying (*who?*) data.[8]

Two questions, then, from Mr. Kipling's bit of verse remain to be considered: *what?* and *why?* We will discover that these two (plus a third, to be discussed in due course) are *basic*[9] questions and must be used constantly by the probing student.

There is a sense in which all of our discussion on

observation and seeing the data is related to this *definitive*[9] question, what. "*What* do I see?" or, "*What* is here?" Certainly after we have noted the terms and the grammatical and literary structure we have had to ask, "*What* is the basic thought of this paragraph?"

Let us consider briefly how this question is used by taking an example. In Mark 10:13-16, we have recorded an incident in the life of our Lord. The student should carefully read the account and make due note of the data: the terms and their structural relationships. Questions will begin to arise in his mind. (Obviously some of the previously discussed questions are significant here as well, but we will limit ourselves to the *what* question.)

"*What* is the meaning of the term 'children'?" (Perhaps you feel this is obvious, but the term can have various meanings according to context, as in 1 John 5:21).

"*What* is the significance of the term 'to Him'?"

"*What* is the force of the verb 'might touch'?"

"*What* is the meaning of the term 'rebuked'?"

"*What* is the antecedent of the pronoun 'this'?"

"*What* is the meaning of the verb 'was indignant'?"

"*What* is the impact of the contrasting structure, 'Let the children come . . . do not hinder them'?"

"*What* is the significance of the term 'belongs'?"

"*What* is the meaning of the term 'kingdom of God'?"

"*What* is the significance of the reduntant expression, 'Truly, I say to . . . '?"

"*What* is the meaning of the term 'whoever'?"

"*What* is the relationship between Jesus' statement in verse 15 and the historical incident'?"

"*What* three things are noted as actions of Jesus towards the children?"

"*What* is meant by the term 'began blessing' in verse 16?"

The student should not for a moment consider that these questions are exhaustive; they simply suggest the way in which we are to raise questions to aid our study.

You can readily see that some of the questions deal with terms, while others are concerned with the structure of the paragraph. It is helpful to distinguish between these two in order to insure that all potential questions are considered. Certainly the student must see the meaning of the terms; but he also must note verb tenses, paragraph relationships, literary structure, etc.

We come next to the question *why*? Here is the most significant of all the questions. It is concerned with the reason behind the statement or action. It provides the maximum insight into the paragraph. It should be noted that this question should also be applied to both terms and structure. Let us turn again to the paragraph in Mark 10. How might we use the question why?

"*Why* were they bringing the children to Jesus?"
"*Why* were they anxious for Jesus to touch them?"
"*Why* did the disciples 'rebuke' the parents?"
"*Why* was Jesus indignant (NASB) with His disciples?" (The NASB does not seem as strong as the AV, "much displeased.")
"*Why* does Jesus state that the kingdom of God belongs to children?"
"*Why* does Jesus use the simile 'like a child' in verse 15?"
"*Why* did Jesus take 'them in his arms' ?"
"*Why* does Jesus lay His hands on them?"

We again caution the student that we are seeking to be suggestive rather than exhaustive. Note how this *rational* [9] question enables the student to gain insights into the basic significance of the passage.

By this time another factor in our procedure should be evident. As you proceed to raise questions, based upon what you have observed in the passage, you will find yourself seeing other things that escaped you earlier. These additional clues must be carefully noted and become, in turn, new material to be subjected to your questioning.

To put it another way, in these early stages of personal Bible study, there is a cyclical pattern that must be recognized. Your observations lead to questions which in turn lead to further observations leading to questions, etc. Viewed graphically, it might look like this:

The procedure must be pursued until the student has exhausted his immediate insights. This is not to suggest that we will exhaust the passage. We must always remember that we are dealing with the Word of God which is "*living* and *active* and sharper than any two-edged sword, and piercing as far as the division of soul and spirit, of both joints and marrow, and able to judge the thoughts and intentions of the heart." [10] We will never plumb the depths of the Word. As we are working on *it*, the Word is working on *us* to bring the will of God to pass in our lives.

Thus we have examined four *subordinate*[8] questions: where? when? how? who? and two *basic*[9] questions: what? why? Perhaps a reminder is in order that the former questions are not to be considered less important than the latter. They are subordinate only because they do not occur in every paragraph.

There remains one basic question that Mr. Kipling does not include in his bit of doggerel verse. I would like to suggest that it might be remembered by the somewhat irreverent phrase "So what?"[11] That is, What does this observation *imply* about the relationships of the people involved? What were the *effects* of the action upon those present? What *relevance* does this have to my contemporary world? Let us see how we might apply the "So what?" question to our passage in Mark 10.

"What is implied about the attitudes of the disciples in this passage?"

"What relationship is implied between Jesus and His disciples here?"

"In what way does this passage reveal the differences in thinking between Jesus and the disciples?"

"What effect do you feel this incident might have had upon the disciples? upon the parents? upon Jesus?"

"What implications come down to us and are applicable in our contemporary world?"

It can readily be seen that this third basic question deals with the wider view of the passage. Indeed the three basic questions are somewhat progressive in their movement. We first ask, "What is the meaning of this term?" Then our query becomes, "Why is this term used?" And finally, "What are the full implications of this term?" Of course the same pattern is followed for observations of grammatical or literary structure.

To sum up this section, we have seen that it is very important for us to develop our ability to ask questions as we study. These should be duly noted and written down as they occur to us. As a guide, the suggestion has been made that we think in terms of three basic questions: what? why? and so what? and four subordinate questions: where? when? how? and who?

The questions are to be applied to terms, structure (both grammatical and literary), paragraph relations, and the emotional tone of the passage.[12]

Several warnings are in order. The most common problem facing the beginning student at this stage is that he is afraid to ask any question for which he does not have an immediate answer. This is obviously self-defeating. We learn nothing if our study simply enables us to rearrange our prejudices.

For the evangelical student this fear stems from one of two sources. The first possible source is pride. He may be afraid to let it be known that there is something that he does not know. This, of course, is simply an evidence of human sin and should be dealt with as such.

The second possible source is a bit more subtle. He may feel that he must protect the Scriptures lest it be discovered that, through his study, an inconsistency or contradiction or error is revealed in Holy Writ. If he feels this way he is admitting that his confidence in the Bible as the Word of God is on pretty shaky ground.

Let us rather recognize that our problems with the Scriptures stem from our inferior knowledge, and that the purpose of all of our study is to increase that knowledge. Open your mind freely to all questions and seek to dispose of them honestly.

A further caution: Be sure to carefully record your questions; don't depend upon your memory. It is well to write them in parallel with your observations. Since all questions grow out of what you see, you should relate them by parallel numbering. Each noted clue will probably give rise to several questions. The following diagram illustrates one satisfactory method:

Verse	Observations	Questions
1:1	1—Note 1	1 (a) Question 1
		(b) Question 2
		(c) Question 3
	2—Note 2	2 (a) Question 1
		(b) Question 2
	3—Note 3	3 (a) Question 1
		(b) Question 2
		(c) Question 3
		(d) Question 4
	etc.	

Questions should be written in full phrases or sentences. If shortcuts are adopted, the student often does not remember what was on his mind when he seeks later to decipher his code.

The art of asking questions is a skill that every Bible student should constantly seek to develop. A questioning mind is a learning mind so long as one stands on the solid foundation of the conviction that the Bible is the infallible, inspired Word of God. Whenever a question comes to which we cannot discover a satisfactory answer, we hold the Scriptures to be correct until further insight and knowledge confirms it. "Rather, let God be found true, though every man be found a liar"! [13]

We will now proceed to find answers to our questions. This is the subject of our next chapter.

But let us first seek to put what we have learned thus far into effect by a few exercises.

EXERCISES FOR CHAPTER 4

Questioning the Data

1. Unit-read chapter 2 of the Gospel of John. Note the paragraph units and their relationships.

2. Carefully note the data evident in the first paragraph (verses 1-11). Record your data as distinct observations, numbered consecutively.

3. Consider each observation carefully, raising all possible questions. Record your questions in parallel with the observations, numbering them so that they are clearly related.

4. Repeat these steps with the remaining three paragraphs.

" '. . . The emotional qualities are antagonistic to clear reasoning. . . . '

" 'I never make exceptions. An exception disproves the rule.' "

—The Sign of the Four

CHAPTER 5

Interpreting the Data

Our hypothetical detective has carefully noted all of the clues and asked the questions suggested by what he has seen. What is his next step? Obviously, he must *interpret* what he has found and seek to come to some conclusions. Thus in Bible study we must now seek to draw conclusions from what we have seen and from the questions we have raised.

There are three basic steps to be followed in interpreting the data: (1) We must find answers to the questions we have raised; (2) we must summarize our material effectively; and (3) we must seek to recreate the passage to make it vivid for our contemporary world. Let us look at each of these in sequence.

1. Answering the Questions

Where do we turn to find answers to our questions? Of course some questions, particularly those related to grammatical structure, may be answered by further examination of the paragraph (e.g., "What is the subject of this verb?" "What is the antecedent of that pronoun?" etc.). But most of our questions should drive us to basic *research tools* for Bible study.

The first tool is one that should already be part of any student's library: a good English *dictionary*. We seriously hinder our growth in understanding by failing to look up words that are not familiar to us. It is not enough to just get a vague idea of the meaning from the context. If a word that is used is strange, it immediately qualifies as an important term and must be dealt with.

The first specialized tool that any Bible student should secure is a good *Bible dictionary*. Used in just the same manner as a regular dictionary, the Bible dictionary defines words and terms that are specifically related to the biblical time period. Even words that seem clear to the student may often yield great reward if pursued in depth.

As an example. when a student reads the second chapter of Mark, he is confronted with the story of the paralytic brought to Jesus by his friends. When they could not get to Him because of the crowd, "they removed the roof above him." [1] (It is interesting that the original text has the force of "they unroofed the roof.") This statement raises some fascinating questions: "How did they get on the roof?" "How could they so easily remove the roof?" "Wasn't this destruction of property?" Ordinarily a student would think that he understood the term "roof," but at this point he should turn to a Bible dictionary to learn something of the way in which houses were constructed in New Testament times. Looking up the word "roof," he might be referred to the word 'house.' He would learn much of the important place of the flat roof in the family life of that time. Many of the roofs were made of large tiles that could be moved back to let in the cooler night air, allowing the heat of the day to dissipate. He would also learn that most of the houses had an outside stairway to the roof, making it possible for the men to carry their friend up with comparatively little difficulty. The use of the Bible dictionary, therefore, gives a much clearer picture of what transpired.

Perhaps one other illustration would be in order. The Scriptures tell us that when Nicodemus and Joseph of Arimathea secured permission to take the body of Jesus for burial, they prepared the body "as is the burial custom of the Jews." [2] A careful student does not simply assume that he knows what the Jewish burial customs were. He goes to his Bible dictionary and looks up the word 'burial' and finds out exactly what was done by the two men.

There are several good Bible dictionaries available today. *The Zondervan Pictorial Bible Dictionary*, edited by Dr. Merrill C. Tenney, is one of the finest. Moody press has published *Unger's Bible Dictionary*, which is also excellent. On an equal par with these is *The New Bible Dictionary* (William B. Eerdmans Publishing Co.). Some of the older Bible dictionaries that have merit are *Smith's Bible Dictionary* and the *Westminster Dictionary of the Bible* (Westminster Press), a dictionary that must be used with care because of some liberal tendencies. A student should secure several of these helps for his personal library.

Closely related to the Bible dictionary is the *Bible handbook*. This tool supplies a good deal of helpful material by way of background for the various books of the Bible. It should be used cautiously so as not to allow it to prejudice the mind as to the outline and contents of the various books. In this regard it has some of the same dangers as Bible commentaries (see below). Two of the best handbooks available today are *Halley's Bible Handbook* (Zondervan) and *Unger's Bible Handbook* (Moody).

The *Bible encyclopedia* is a more complete work than a Bible dictionary. Often more bibliographic material is included as well as a much more adequate treatment of the various topics. While there are some smaller works available, the finest Bible encyclopedia is *The International Standard Bible Encyclopedia* in five volumes (Eerdmans), commonly referred to as ISBE. The student may, of course, consult this in a library, but it would be a valuable possession for one's personal library.

A further tool that each student should possess is a good *Bible atlas*. Often as one works in a passage he is confronted with geographic data such as locations, terrain (mountains, valleys, etc.), climatic conditions, etc. He should have available to him a source book that will enable him to answer the "where?" and other related questions. Every town and city mentioned in the text should be located on a map so that the student may develop an accurate perspective and a sense of geographic proportion.

In telling the story of the Good Samaritan, Jesus began by saying, "A certain man *was going down* from Jerusalem to Jericho." [3] The student must ask himself, "What is the meaning of the word 'down'?" Was Jesus stating that Jericho was south of Jerusalem? It is essential to find out geographical facts about the two cities. A check with a Bible atlas quickly establishes the fact that Jericho was slightly to the northeast of Jerusalem at a distance of about eight miles. However, the significant discovery is that Jerusalem was 2,500 feet above sea level, while Jericho was located 800 feet *below* sea level. Therefore in a distance of eight miles the traveller descended 3,300 feet! Little wonder that the journey from Jericho to Jerusalem was considered a six-hour journey.[4]

Similarly, Jesus is often referred to as going "*up to Jerusalem.*" [5] When His starting point was in Galilee, one glance at the map will show that He was going due south. Would it not be proper to say that He was going *down* to Jerusalem? Not if you were a native of Palestine. The elevation of Jerusalem was such that, regardless of the direction from which you approached, you always had quite a climb to reach the Holy City (*Mt. Zion*). Any native of New England is familiar with the expression, going "down to Maine"! If you reside somewhere else and are limited to a map, you would of course go *up* to Maine. But the New Englander knows that when you move from the Green and White Mountains of western New England to the coast of Maine, you are going *down*.

Some of the good Bible atlases available today are *The Zondervan Pictorial Bible Atlas*, edited by E. M. Blaiklock (Zondervan); *The Wycliffe Historical Geography of Bible Lands*, edited by Charles F. Pfeiffer and Howard F. Vos (Moody), and *Baker's Bible Atlas* (Baker Book House).

Another helpful aid for the Bible student is a good *Bible introduction*. The purpose of this work is to provide background for the various books, discussing such matters as authorship, date of writing, reason for writing, the people to whom the book was addressed, etc. The historical setting of the particular Bible book being studied is often presented so that the student can gain the maximum benefit from his study. The student is urged to avoid depending on such works for outlines and interpretations. One's own study can often be prejudiced by reading someone else's conclusions before doing his own work.

Several of the good introductions that are available today include: *A General Introduction to the Bible* by Geisler and Nix (Moody, 1968); *The New Bible Survey* by J. Lawrence Eason (Zondervan, 1963); and *General Biblical Introduction* by H. S. Miller (The Word-Bearer Press).

A *concordance* is a must for the Bible student. We mention it here since we are discussing the Bible student's 'tool chest,' even though its most important function comes considerably later in our procedure. This work enables the student to find a verse when he cannot remember the reference but can recall some of the key words. Although a limited concordance is often included at the back of many Bible editions, the serious student should consider securing an exhaustive concordance as soon as possible.

The three most common concordances in use today are usually identified by their authors: *Young's* (Eerdmans); *Strong's* (Abingdon Press); and *Cruden's* (Zondervan). The first two are very large volumes, but they include every use of every word in the Scriptures. For a more concise (and therefore somewhat limited) work, the beginning student might consider *The New Combined Bible Dictionary and Concordance* by Charles F. Pfeiffer (Baker, 1965).

The student can gain much benefit from many other works which we might categorize as *background books*. The student would do well to keep on the lookout for competent works that will provide insight into the history, geography, and culture of Bible times. Outstanding in this area would be the works of Alfred Edersheim. His two-volume *Life and Times of Jesus the Messiah* (Eerdmans) should rank high on the priority list of anyone interested in building a strong library for Bible study. In addition, his two smaller works, *Sketches of Jewish Social Life in the Time of Christ* (Eerdmans) and *The Temple: Its Ministry and Services* (Eerdmans), are extremely helpful in providing insight into first-century cultural patterns.

The student should keep alert to obtaining material of this type that will provide adequate answers to the questions that he should be raising from the inductive study of the passage.

Perhaps the reader is now asking, "But what about *commentaries?*" Many times the student is urged to purchase the works of some of the great Bible teachers and learn what they have to say about the Scriptures. These will range from one volume commentaries on the whole Bible to large multi-volumed sets.

With just a little thought one can understand that the reading of commentaries is contradictory to *personal* Bible study. When you turn to the thoughts and ideas of another, even though he be an outstanding Bible teacher, you will find that you will be seeing the Word through *his* eyes; your mind will be set to see things only as he does.

To the extent that you limit yourself to the background material that the author presents, you will find that the commentary can have as much value as any other background book. But when you read the author's *conclusions*, you hinder your own ability to see the passage for yourself.

The great value of the commentary comes after you have completely finished your study. *Then* you can go to the commentary to see if your conclusions agree with the author's. If they do not, read his arguments and see if he can convince you that you have missed something. If he does not convince you, you are obligated to maintain your convictions on the basis of your own study.

Thus far in this chapter we have been suggesting

sources to which the student can go in order to find answers to his questions. Perhaps we should consider a few practical methods to utilize these answers. The answers should be written down and directly related to the questions. The student might use three parallel columns as shown below:

Verse	Observations	Questions	Answers
1:1	1. Observation No. 1	1 (a) Question 1	1 (a) Answer 1
		(b) Question 2	
		(c) Question 3	2 (b) Answer 2
			3 (c) Answer 3

As suggested in the diagram, the answers often taken considerably more room than the questions. An alternate plan then would be to continue the two parallel columns for the observations and questions and use the reverse of the page for the answers to the questions. It is very important to maintain accurate numbering so that the student can readily relate the answer to the question.

As the answers are recorded it is wise to indicate the source from which the answer was secured. The student can devise his own code to indicate the work and then give the page number. For example, if the *International Standard Bible Encyclopedia* was the source for a particular answer, the student could use this code: ISBE, p. 1250. The purpose of this should be obvious. There may be some reason to go back and verify the answer that you have given. This would be impossible if the source were not noted.

The first step in interpretation has now been completed: answering the questions. We are ready to proceed to the next step. The student has now gained valuable insights: the terms have become clear and the incidents have become much more vivid and real in his mind. The Bible is much fresher and alive to him. What next?

2. Summarizing the Material

It is time to summarize what has been found. This is where the loose ends are brought together. We have been working from the parts to the whole. Now we must put it all together. In effect, what we are doing now is saying, "This is what I have discovered." There are various ways of doing this.

We are now ready to *name the paragraphs* and then to develop our paragraph names (or titles) to capture the heart of each paragraph. Titles may be either declarative (full sentences) or topical (phrases). They may be concerned with content (summary) or meaning (interpretive). It is well for the student to stay with one type or the other in a given section. Perhaps he will be helped by trying to give both summary and interpretive titles to the paragraphs in a given section.

To illustrate, let us take the twelve paragraphs that make up the first two chapters of John. We will give them both summary and interpretive titles.

	SUMMARY	INTERPRETIVE
1:1-5	The Word of God	The Essential Word
1:6-8	John, The Witness	Witness to the Word
1:9-13	The Light Which Enlightens	The Enlightening Word
1:14-18	The Word Made Flesh	The Incarnate Word
1:19-28	The Interrogation of John	John Under Fire
1:29-34	The Sign of the Baptism	Divine Seal of Approval
1:35-42	Finding the Messiah	Divine Hospitality Offered
1:43-51	Call of Philip and Nathaniel	Divine Promise of Wonders

2:1-11	Water to Wine	Divine Power Demonstrated
2:12	Sojourn in Capernaum	
2:13-22	Cleansing the Temple	Divine Authority Expressed
2:23-25	Noncommitment to Men	Divine Knowledge of Men

It can readily be seen that I have elected to use topical titles here. It can be equally as effective to use declarative titles (complete sentences) should the student wish.

Under no circumstances should the student think that these are the titles that should be used! They are simply suggestive and illustrative. The student should develop his own titles always. To adopt the titles of someone else is to fail to engage in *personal* Bible study.

The next step is to group those paragraphs which belong together and develop titles for each section.

Outlining the passage is an excellent way of summarizing. You will recall that in the very beginning, moving from the whole to the parts, we made a tentative outline. We know a great deal more now, so we can be much more confident in our outline.

The student should beware of using someone else's outline. As much as you admire a certain professor or Bible teacher, don't be satisfied with adopting his work as your own. The outline should be *your* summary of what *you* feel the passage is saying.

One of the best ways to bring together what you have discovered is to develop a *summary chart*[6] of the book that you have been studying. This enables you to get all of the pertinent material down in clear, concise graphic form where it can be seen quickly.

There are many possible variations to charting and the student is urged to exercise his originality at this point. It might be helpful to suggest the wisdom of putting your final chart on the inside of a manila folder. You then have the complete chart of the book at hand, and can use the folder to file pertinent information, clippings, illustrations, etc., that pertain to that book.

The *vertical chart* is an excellent way of graphically recording your outline:

```
I. - - - - - - - - - - - - - - - - - - - - - - - - - - - - - - - - - - - - - - -
   A. - - - - - - - - - - - - - - - - - - - - - - - - - - - - - - - - - - - - -
      1. - - - - - - - - - - - - - - - - - - - - - - - - - - - - - - - - - - -
      2. - - - - - - - - - - - - - - - - - - - - - - - - - - - - - - - - - - -
   B. - - - - - - - - - - - - - - - - - - - - - - - - - - - - - - - - - - - - -
      1. - - - - - - - - - - - - - - - - - - - - - - - - - - - - - - - - - - -
      2. - - - - - - - - - - - - - - - - - - - - - - - - - - - - - - - - - - -

II. - - - - - - - - - - - - - - - - - - - - - - - - - - - - - - - - - - - - - -

III. - - - - - - - - - - - - - - - - - - - - - - - - - - - - - - - - - - - - -
```

Another method of charting is the *horizontal chart:*

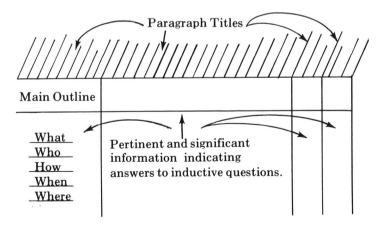

There are certain advantages to the horizontal chart. It allows for more flexibility and certainly makes it possible to include more information than the vertical chart. Also, the use of color and suggestive sketches can make the chart more attractive and easier to read.

Again, the student is urged to use his creativity and imagination in charting the results of his study. He will benefit immeasurably by having a permanent, useful and attractive aid both for further study and for teaching the material to others.

The student is urged, in every case, to use these first three methods of summary: paragraph titles, the outline, the chart. However, there are additional methods that may prove useful for certain materials.

When the passage is quite involved and detailed, it may be wise to *list the main truths*. This would be done by way of preliminary summary in preparation for the other techniques.

Occasionally the student may feel that it would be helpful to *paraphrase the section*. The paraphrase is simply a restatement of the same ideas in different words. Such a technique might prove to be quite useful in the case of a passage like Romans 7, where a rapid reading of the English (especially in the KJV) leaves one with a feeling of frustration, as though he were hearing double-talk.

We have now dealt with the first two stages of our interpreting of the data: answering the questions and summarizing the material. There remains one further step: we must *recreate* the passage. That is, we must take the results of all of our study and seek to relive the passage and make it excitingly contemporary. This is really the heart of interpretation.

3. Recreating the Passage

In order to *recreate* the passage effectively, we must learn to practice total empathy. That is, we must actually put ourselves into the position of the characters in the narrative and relive the experience. On the basis of all of the material that we have researched, we become part of the story.

How can one illustrate empathy? Watch a young mother as she spoon feeds her baby. At a time like that the focus of attention is usually on the baby. But watch the mother: you will discover that she is opening her mouth just as she wants her baby to do. She is empathizing with her child.

The word 'empathy' literally means "to feel within," to vicariously experience the feelings of another. Take any biblical narrative; imagine yourself as one of the characters, then another. Relive the incident until it is as vivid as contemporary life.

An excellent way to learn to empathize is to use the learning technique known as *psychodrama*. Describing the basic outlines of a situation, several people then seek to act and speak as they imagine the actual person might act and speak. Imagine yourself as the little boy whose lunch Jesus used to feed the 5,000; try to relive the day up to that incident.

It is obvious that the second factor in recreation is an imagination, controlled and guided by the Holy Spirit. You must project yourself back into the situation, sensing and feeling the atmosphere.

Let us take a little exercise in spiritual imagination. Stand with those mourners in the little garden cemetery outside of Bethany;[7] the Lord is the center of attention. Some are wondering why He didn't come earlier; some, out of sympathy for the sisters, Mary and Martha, feel even a bit bitter toward Jesus.

Jesus speaks: "Remove the stone!" A shock wave goes through the group. Many agree with Martha when she protests the possibility of unpleasantness at the odor of the decomposing body. Jesus reminds her of His earlier statement, "If you believe, you will see the glory of God." Can you sense the wonder, the tension of the crowd?

Now the stone is removed. Is there an odor? What do you see in the blackness of the cave? Jesus speaks loudly: "Lazarus, come forth!" Do you sense the crowd collectively catching its breath? Suddenly a figure appears; wrapped in bulky grave clothes, not walking (the Scripture clearly tells us he was "bound hand and foot") but moving mysteriously to the entrance! (Perhaps at this point some in the crowd take off! This is too much for them!)

Jesus speaks again: "Unbind him, and let him go!" Who moves first? Watch closely. Who in that little circle would step forward to begin removing the grave clothes? Isn't it Mary? Don't you sense that she, of all those present, would rush to the cave? And what does she do first? She removes the face cloth from his head,[8] slowly, tenderly, then drops it and exclaims triumphantly, "He's alive! He's alive!" for she looks into the sparkling, seeing eyes of her brother! Now others rush forward to help. The grave clothes are removed and a robe is brought. Lazarus, dead four days, is restored to his sisters.

Fanciful, you say? But could it not actually have happened that way? As you learn to *feel* the passage, you can begin to *recreate* it.

When recreating material other than narrative, you must still seek to identify with both writer and reader, striving to think and express your thoughts in parallel with theirs. As you read the little Epistle to Philemon, make a conscious attempt to think as Paul thought; then become Philemon seeking to act on Paul's request to take back his slave as a brother in Christ; and finally put yourself in the place of Onesimus.

The basic principle behind all of our recreation is that man has not changed. His culture, his behavior patterns, his likes and dislikes—all vary from region to region and from generation to generation. But man himself remains the same. He loves his children, has fears and frustrations, seeks to go his own way, expresses himself in pettiness and anger, yet is capable of responding to the revelation of God. As you seek to relive the Scripture, ask yourself, "How would I feel?" and you will be fairly close to the feeling of the man who originally lived the incident.

We have now seen what is in the passage; we have raised questions and sought out the answers; we have empathized with the men and women of the Bible and have sought to recreate the passage and make it live. This is interpretation.

Let us consider several exercises to help us to apply what has been discussed.

EXERCISES FOR CHAPTER 5

Interpreting the Data

1. Carefully unit-read the four paragraphs of John 3.
2. Develop a worksheet of observations and questions. Make an effort to research the most important questions,

and record your answers as fully as possible.

3. Summarize the results of your study by giving paragraph titles to the paragraphs and making a chart of the unit.

4. Make a conscious effort to empathize both with Jesus and Nicodemus. Recreate the scene as though you were standing by watching. Describe it in your own words.

" 'You will not apply my precept,' he said, shaking his head. 'How often have I said to you that when you have eliminated the impossible, whatever remains, however improbable, *must be the truth?...*' "
—The Sign of the Four

"*I knew that seclusion and solitude were very necessary for my friend in those hours of intense mental concentration during which he weighed every particle of evidence, constructed alternative theories, balanced one against the other, and made up his mind as to which points were essential and which immaterial.*"
—The Hound of the Baskervilles

"*The temptation to form premature theories upon insufficient data is the bane of our profession.*"
—The Valley of Fear

"*Sherlock Holmes was a man, however, who when he had an unsolved problem upon his mind would go for days, and even for a week, without rest, turning it over, rearranging his facts, until he had either fathomed it, or convinced himself that the data was insufficient.*"
—The Man with the Twisted Lip

CHAPTER 6

Testing the Data

Once our friend the detective has arrived at his interpretation of the clues and has reconstructed (summarized) the events of the crime, there is a further essential step that he must take. It is necessary to *test* his conclusions by every means possible. It is a serious matter to accuse someone falsely of a crime. The detective had better be very sure that he is right!

So it is with our interpretation of the Scriptures; we want to be certain that our conclusions are valid. None of us would want to be guilty of saying, "Thus saith the Lord," and then be wrong!

There are two principal ways in which we test our conclusions: (1) We check very carefully within the paragraph, then within the section, the division, the book, to see that our conclusions are *internally* valid. (2) We seek to *correlate* what we have found with other portions of scripture dealing with the same or similar themes. Let us consider these further.

1. Internal Validity

Perhaps we have this problem in Bible study more than in any other field of learning. It is a constant source of amazement how people seem to delight in finding the peculiar, the odd, or the unusual in the Scriptures without seeking to ask, "Does the passage really mean that?"

In a probably apocryphal story, someone has said that the reason why the four men who sought to bring their paralytic friend to Jesus were unable to get to Him was because of the large number of newspapermen present. In disbelief one turns to Mark 2:4 (KJV) and reads, "They could not come nigh unto him for the *press. . . .* " Another has claimed that Jesus surely could heal "the bends" (an affliction that affects those who rise too quickly from the depths of the sea, without permitting their bodies to adjust to variations of pressure), because Luke 4:40 (KJV) states, "All they that had any sick with *divers diseases* brought them unto him; and he laid his hands on every one of them, and healed them."

We can readily see that we test our conclusions by applying common sense to our study. We dare not cheapen God by involving Him in that which is patently absurd or ludicrous.

However, let us hasten to add that this does not mean that we seek to explain away the miraculous in the Scriptures. The skeptic who rejects the supernatural and claims that the miracles of our Lord were the imaginations of the later church ascribed to Jesus to suggest that He was more than a man, has absolutely no basis for his position. He himself becomes absurd.

Consider the attempt of the recent fiction writer to rule out the miraculous account of Jesus walking on the water:

The Hebrew word *al* was always translated as *on*, so that the Scriptures tell us that Jesus walked *on* the water. However, the Hebrew word *al* also has another meaning, which is *by*. Therefore, the translations could have as correctly read that Jesus walked *by* the water, in short, took a stroll by the seaside. But perhaps the early Christian propagandists deliberately sought a miracle worker instead of a pedestrian.[1]

The student of the Scriptures smiles at such foolishness and wonders what it was that Peter sank into and in which he feared that he would drown![2]

This is no different from an earlier novelist's attempt to explain the miracle of Jesus' feeding the 5,000:

> . . . The old man had drifted back to his memories of the remarkable feast in the desert.
>
> "The boy must have been sitting at the Master's feet," he soliloquized, with averted eyes. "He must have been sitting there all the time; for when Jesus said we would now eat our supper, there he was—as if he had popped up from nowhere—holding out his little basket."
>
> It had taken Bartholomew a long time to tell of that strange supper: *the sharing of bread*, the new acquaintances, the breaking down of reserve among strangers, the tenderness toward the old one and the little ones . . . .[3]

Nothing here of blessing and breaking and multiplying the loaves and fish; just a suggestion that those who had their lunch shared it with those who did not. No miracle, just a happy picnic.

Illustrations of this sort of thing abound. One of the writer's professors was fond of reporting about the liberal scholar who sought to explain the phenomenon of the floating axehead during the lifetime of the prophet Elisha.[4] This so-called scholar explained the account by suggesting that the axehead probably fell on the back of a turtle dozing at the bottom of the river. Disturbed by the weight of the axehead, the turtle rose, just as Elisha got there, so that the young man could reach out and take the axehead again.

In no way are we seeking to explain away the wonders of the Word! Rather we are seeking to use sanctified common sense to be sure of what the Scriptures are saying.

Let us consider a more serious illustration. In Psalm 116 the psalmist says, "I shall lift up the cup of salvation, and call upon the name of the Lord." [5] Just what does he mean by "the cup of salvation"? In pondering this, the student certainly would note that the psalmist describes his salvation experience in verses 1-8. It does not seem that he would be talking about that again here. What then?

A cup, of course, is a vessel to contain something. What kind of vessel is it that contains salvation? Certainly the Word of God does! Consider Romans 10:17, "Faith comes from hearing, and hearing by the word of Christ." The Lord Jesus said, "Heaven and earth will pass away, but My words shall not pass away." [6] Could this passage be a determination to take up the Word of God and read it regularly? Is the psalmist saying that because of his love for the Lord he will read his Word faithfully? Can the believer of today see here an exhortation to faithfulness in daily devotions? Possibly so, but is this what the psalmist meant? He probably had little of the written Scriptures available to him.

We proceed then to *test* our suggested conclusion. We study the passage and see that it could fit internally. The psalmist is telling us several things that he is covenanting to do because he loves the Lord. There remains a bit of uncertainty, however.

We must go beyond the test of internal validity to the second step.

2. External Comparison

External comparison[7] is the procedure of going outside of the passage to other portions of Scripture that use the same term or deal with the same subject.

This step is most clearly seen when we compare similar accounts from the several Gospel records. We see the story as described by each of the authors and discover that each one supplements the others, supplying details that are lacking elsewhere. All four Gospels record the miracle of the feeding of the 5,000; but only Mark tells us that the grass on which the crowd sat was green! [8]

But we must also make the effort to compare similar uses of terms. Let us return to our illustration. We are seeking to discover what the psalmist means by the term "cup of salvation." Can we find other uses of this term? In Psalm 16:5 the poet exclaims, "The Lord is the portion of my inheritance and my *cup* ... " And again in the very familiar 23rd psalm, "My *cup* overflows." Obviously, then, the term 'cup' has considerable figurative use.

We return to our Bible dictionary or encyclopedia for help and discover that the suggestion is made that this phrase might have reference to the libation cup of praise lifted in thanksgiving in connection with certain of the sacrifices.[9] Professor Delitzsch states, "The cup of salvation is that which is raised aloft and drunk amid thanks for the manifold and rich salvation already experienced ... The poet is thinking of the sacrificial meal in connection with the ... thank-offering, at which meal the offerers ate and drank in a grateful, joyous mood." [10]

Our conclusion, then, may well be that the psalmist is saying in effect, "Because I love the Lord I am going to express my gratitude in praise and thanksgiving to Him."

What is it that we have done? We have taken our preliminary conclusions and subjected them to the test. We have first considered the internal validity of our conclusion and then considered the external comparison to determine the probable meaning of our passage.

One further thing should be said in the matter of testing the data. Our test might take us to extrabiblical sources, other written materials of the same period that might use phrases or terms that are used in the scriptural record.

For many years it was believed that the New Testament was written in a special Spirit-directed language. There were so many differences between the Greek of the Scriptures and the literary language of the period that the conclusion seemed inevitable that it was a unique medium. Then the archeologists discovered many fragments of writing, both on papyrus and on broken pieces of pottery, that demonstrated conclusively that the language of the Word of God was the ordinary everyday language of the people. The same vocabulary was used in the Gospel of Mark that would be used on a grocery list prepared by a mother for her household.

For this reason the Greek of the New Testament is referred to as the Koine (or "common") Greek. This means that we can find parallels of word usage and meaning from these very papyri. Where a word might be used two or three times in the Scriptures, we might find a number of uses in materials external to the Bible.

Naturally, many of these discoveries are not available to the student who is unable to use the Greek. However, some of the fine books by Dr. Kenneth Wuest[11] and other writers do provide insights for the student who is restricted to the English.

The basic tool for this step of testing the data is the concordance. Here is the aid that enables us to locate further uses of a given term, or parallel accounts of the same event. By utilizing one of the more complete concordances, such as Young's or Strong's, it is possible to pinpoint every use of a given term in the Scriptures. We can then make comparative studies to verify or to discard the conclusions to which we have arrived in our previous study.

We have now examined the data thoroughly, both from the whole to the parts, and from the parts to the whole; we have questioned the data and sought by research to find answers to our questions so that we might interpret the data; we have summarized the data carefully and then subjected all of it to careful testing. Now we are ready to move to the final step of our process. In many respects, this last step is the most important of all. But before we turn to it, let us consider certain exercises that will help to crystallize our work thus far.

EXERCISES FOR CHAPTER 6

Testing the Data

1. Make a complete personal study of the eight paragraphs of John 6. Follow the procedure as outlined in our previous study.

2. Two of these paragraphs record accounts found in the other Gospels. Make a comparative study to discover

details and information supplied by the various accounts. Note particularly how the passage in John amplifies the teaching which Jesus gave.

3. Note particularly how John uses the technique of climax in this portion. Can you trace the increasing tension through the segment? What significance do you give to this?

" 'On the contrary, Watson, you can see everything. You fail, however, to reason from what you see. You are too timid in drawing your inferences."
—The Adventure of the Blue Carbuncle

"I have already explained to you that what is out of the common is usually a guide rather than a hindrance."
—A Study in Scarlet

CHAPTER 7

Applying the Data

The detective is ready to make his arrest; and we are ready to take the scriptures which we have studied and come to grips with the problems of everyday life.

Everyone is anxious to apply scripture. How many Sunday school teachers last Sunday read a verse or paragraph from the Bible to the class and then proceeded to say, "Now this means—"? Or, perhaps the teacher read the passage and said to the pupils, "Now what do you think this means?" and everyone's opinion was considered with equal weight as though the significance was to be discovered in a consensus of the opinions of sincere people.

The Lord can sometimes use this method, but one wonders if it is not in spite of its naivety rather than because of its effectiveness. A friend, who today is a minister of the gospel, was saved while serving in the Navy. A few days after his conversion he boarded a ship for the Mediterranean. He posted a notice saying that there would be a Bible class. Quite a few of the crew showed up, but none knew anything about the Bible. They decided that they should read the New Testament, starting at the beginning, each one reading a verse and then commenting on what he thought it meant. They turned to Matthew and read, "Abraham begat Isaac; and Isaac begat Jacob. . . . " They labored through the first 17 verses. When they arrived at verse 18, someone sighed and said, "Now we're at it!" The text read, "Now the birth of Jesus Christ was on this wise."

The amazing and wonderful corollary to the story is that at the end of that particular cruise there were fifteen new Christians among that crew! The Lord honored His Word even though it was stumblingly presented.

Let us not assume, therefore, that application is easily done! All that we have been suggesting by way of method must precede this step. We must carefully examine the data, raise our questions, seek our answers, summarize our conclusions, and put our findings to the test. Only then are we ready to *apply*.

But even so there are certain qualifications necessary if we are to apply the Scriptures effectively. It is conceivable that one may be a careful student of the Scriptures and yet not be very capable in applying those same Scriptures to life.

Certainly the individual must have a basic *reverence* for God and His Word. The Word of God is not to be used as a club, to beat people into submission to the will of the preacher; nor is it to be wielded as a sword to slay the opposition. The Bible likens itself to a sword, but its operation is internal, laying a man open before God, revealing motives and intentions so that "there is no creature hidden from His sight . . . " [1]

The preacher or teacher who uses the Bible in order to get people to do *his* will is in serious danger of committing a type of blasphemy: setting himself up as God.

This brings us to a second essential in the makeup

of the man who would effectively apply the Word: *humility*. Such an elusive trait! It has been said that humility is that trait of character which, as soon as you know you have it, you've lost it! There are those who flaunt their humility, who are proud that they are humble! Strange contradiction this! The truly humble person thinks not of himself at all. He is too enraptured in his love for the Lord Jesus Christ and His Word to give himself a thought. He cries out with Paul, "May it never be that I should boast, except in the cross of our Lord Jesus Christ, through which the world has been crucified to me, and I to the world." [2]

A further trait essential in the makeup of the one who is to sincerely apply the Word of God is that of true *Christian love*. There is a sense in which this characteristic is the natural outgrowth of the other two. Certainly reverence and humility must be present in the person who demonstrates genuine New Testament love.

The preacher of the gospel who truly loves his people will not hesitate to apply *all* of the Scriptures, not just that which will be pleasing to his congregation. Love that divorces itself from essential discipline is not love, but indulgence. We need to appropriate the apostle's words to Timothy, "All Scripture is inspired by God and profitable for teaching, for reproof, for correction, for training in righteousness; that the man of God may be adequate, equipped for every good work." [3]

Notice that the Word is meant not only for teaching, but also for reproof and correction; training implies restraints and direction. And all of this must be done with a loving regard for the Lord and His children.

Christian love also demands that a man come

to deeply understand his people; he must know the forces that play upon them, the pressures that cause them to act as they do. We cannot excuse and overlook sin, but we can make a conscientious effort to understand the sinner.

Reverence, humility, Christian love—these are the prerequisites in applying scripture. Obviously these are subjective factors; they have to do with the outlook and attitude of the one who is called upon to do the applying. But there are also some objective factors to be considered with reference to the Scriptures themselves.

"All Scripture is ... profitable. ... " But is every portion of scripture equally applicable to every situation? Does the same passage reprove and comfort at the same time? Is it not true that, given a specific situation, the task of the Bible expositor is to bring into focus that passage which best meets the need? that most adequately provides the required guidance?

In order to do this the student of the Word must consider the *relevance* of the passage he is studying. More specifically, he must consider whether the passage is local or universal, and whether it is temporary or timeless. Further, he must determine the realm of experience for which the given passage might be used. Let us consider each of these in turn.

(1) *Local or universal.* The early chapters of the book of Acts record the fascinating history of the early days of the Church. One aspect that the Bible student notices of the early church is that "all things were common property to them." [4] Are we, then, to conclude, as some have, that scripture teaches "Christian communism"? In very recent days a communal type of Christianity is being urged upon Christians as the fulfillment of the biblical pattern. But is this so?

We can look in vain throughout the rest of the book of Acts and through the Epistles for any such injunction. Nowhere (not even in Jerusalem) were the believers urged to practice this. So far as can be determined it was a spontaneous expression of love in the Jerusalem church growing out of the *local* situation. Many people had received the Lord, among them some whose livelihood depended upon the "welfare programs" of the temple! This seemed like the most loving solution to the *local* problems.

Of course we are to see the universal principle: we are to be concerned for our brother and be prepared to help him in love.[5] But the specifics are concerned with a local situation.

Compare this with the Great Commission from our Lord: "All authority has been given to Me in Heaven and on earth. Go therefore and make disciples of all the nations, baptizing them in the name of the Father and the Son and the Holy Spirit, teaching them to observe all that I command you . . . "[6] There is nothing local here; it is a universal command from our Master.

(2) *Temporary or timeless*. The eleventh chapter of First Corinthians contains a rather involved argument concerning the need for a woman to have her head covered when worshipping. Until fairly recently this was considered a mark of true piety. But are we correct in concluding that this was an instruction for all times and cultures? Again in chapter 14 we read, "Let the women keep silent in the churches; for they are not permitted to speak. . . . "[7] Is this to be followed in its entirety today? Are we to eliminate our feminine Sunday school teachers? Are we to ask our ladies not to participate in a testimony meeting?

In order to accurately apply this passage, we must know something of the culture of first-century Corinth. Our background studies reveal the gross immorality so evident in this cosmopolitan city. We learn that so many details of behavior had to be carefully controlled lest the church and the Lord Jesus Christ be disgraced. For a woman to appear in public with her head uncovered, or for that same woman to be seen publicly speaking with men, was to advertise the fact that she was available for immoral purposes. How important that the women in the church scrupulously guard against any such interpretation being placed on their actions!

We can see then that the details were temporary, that is, that they had supreme relevance to the situation in Corinth. Nevertheless there is a timeless principle here: We are not to engage in any activity that will bring disgrace to the Name of our Lord and to the ministry of His church.

(3) *The realm of experience.* Once we have carefully determined what is universal and timeless in the passage, we then want to bring it to bear upon the contemporary situation in which we find ourselves. The way in which we do this is to determine the realm of experience to which a given passage is applicable.

When we make our study of a portion, we should seek to consider how we might use it. Is this a passage that might bring comfort to someone who is ill or bereaved? Does this section present the way of salvation in a particularly clear way so that we might use it with an inquirer? Is this a unit that can reassure the person who may have doubts about his salvation? Perhaps the skeptic can be convinced effectively by the study of this passage.

Whatever the circumstances, there is a portion of the Word of God that can bring help, guidance and satisfaction. The task is for those of us who are students of the Word to bring the Word thoughtfully to bear upon the situation.

What are the guidelines to remember? How do we go about applying the Scripture?

First of all, we apply it *personally*. We have no business seeking to get others to follow injunctions in the Scriptures which we are not willing to put into practice in our own lives. The pastor who urges his people to give a tithe of their income to the work of the Lord, but who does not do so himself, is not deserving of a hearing. He may rationalize and excuse himself, saying, "Well, I'm in the Lord's work; therefore whatever I have is being used in the Lord's work." This is so much sophistry! Don't ask your people to do what you are not willing to do.

One of the concerns that weighs heavily on the heart of anyone who seeks to teach future Christian workers lies just in this area. Young men who in a few short years will be urging their parishioners to attend the prayer meeting, do not themselves attend the prayer meeting in a local church during their student days. Often students feel that they are exempt from the biblical admonitions about giving. "I need every cent I get in order to pay my school bills," they say. But giving is not relative to what you need; it is relative to what you have! If the members of a local assembly began to give only after all of their bills were paid, the church would receive very little. The student who is not involved in teaching a Sunday school class may find himself excusing his nonattendance at the Sunday school!

Wherever you find a command or injunction in the Scriptures, apply it to yourself first. Only then have you earned the right to apply it to someone else.

The next thing to remember is that we should apply it *lovingly*. There is no place for the tyrant, the whip, or the chastening rod in the work of the Lord. Remember, the Word says, "Whom the Lord loves He disciplines, and He scourges every son whom He receives." [8] But it is the *Lord* who does the scourging! Our task is to point out the teachings of the Scriptures, seek to follow them ourselves, and in love urge others to do so.

The great danger of the Christian worker is the peril of self-righteousness. The religious leaders of Jesus' day thought they were serving God, yet they became the "betrayers and murderers" [9] of the Son of God. Whenever the student of the Word begins to think he is superior to someone else, he is in grave peril. Apply the Word personally and lovingly.

A third principle to maintain is the importance of applying the Word of God *consistently*. There must not be one application for friends and another for strangers. Nor can we teach that the Word gave certain instruction that was applicable yesterday but does not apply today. The basic teachings of the Scriptures are timeless and universal. We may need to learn more of the culture or thought patterns of the people to whom we go in order to understand them, but having done so, the Word of God is just as applicable to the Australian aborigine as it is to the Oxford professor.

Cultures vary in a fascinating manner. Man has devised many solutions to the problems of meeting his basic needs. But wherever you find him, he is *man*—the apex of the creation of God, created in the Image of God—and the Word of God applies to him. The Lord Jesus told us to "go into all the world and preach the gospel to all creation. He who has believed and has been baptized shall be saved; but he who has disbelieved shall be condemned." [10] We must be consistent in our application of the Word.

Other admonitions could be given, but the last we shall include is that we be sure to apply the Word *thoroughly*. It is amazing how we wish to accept only what is pleasant to us and reject that which we may not like. This we dare not do! *All* Scripture is profitable; *all* must be proclaimed. The preacher should carefully plan his preaching to include all sections of the Bible. The student must expose his own life to the entire Word so that he does not ignore the holiness of Leviticus as he seeks to embrace the activism of Acts.

Thus do we conclude the steps involved in *personal* Bible study. The system is complete. It remains only for us to put it into practice diligently. As we conscientiously do so, remembering that whatever effort and time we put into it is supremely worthwhile, the Word of God should become more vibrant, vital, and dynamic to us than it ever was before. We should learn the experience of Jeremiah who, when he was so discouraged that he was tempted to give up, said:

> If I say, "I will not remember Him
> Or speak any more in His Name,"
> Then in my heart it becomes like a burning fire
> Shut up in my bones;
> And I am weary of holding it in,
> And I cannot endure it.[11]

What was it that was "like a burning fire"? It was "the Word of the Lord." So, too, every student of the Word can experience the fire of the Word in his life.

EXERCISES FOR CHAPTER 7

Applying the Data

1. Carefully meditate on what you have learned from the early chapters of John. Enumerate the spiritual lessons that you see in these chapters.

2. List the things that you see that are local and temporary as contrasted with those things that are universal and timeless.

3. To what areas of experience do you feel these paragraphs speak? Be specific.

4. From these chapters, what applications do you feel you can make to our contemporary world?

CHAPTER 8

Poetry, Parable and Prophecy

Our methodology has now been completed. Hopefully, the student will take the step-by-step procedure as it has been presented and proceed to spend the rest of his life becoming skillful in interpreting the Word of God, "not walking in craftiness or adulterating the word of God, but by the manifestation of truth commending [himself] to every man's conscience in the sight of God." [1]

It remains for something to be said about the several types of biblical literature that present unique problems to the student. It is not to be suggested that in a brief chapter such as this we can present all of the ramifications of these; but we can, perhaps, give some guidelines that will prove to be helpful in interpreting and applying the portions of the Word where these forms are used.

1. Poetry

Let us consider first the *poetry* of the Scriptures. It will readily be seen that we are discussing Hebrew poetry, since the authors of any poetry found in the Word were Hebrews. We need to consider the unique characteristics of this poetry as compared to the verse patterns in our English language.

There are a few similar features. Poetry in every language seeks to communicate *feeling*. The poet is not so much trying to get you to know what he knows as he is seeking to get you to feel as he feels. Read thoughtfully the 29th psalm several times and see if you can't *feel* the presence of the Lord in a storm as the psalmist does. (Perhaps you will never again be fearful when overtaken by a storm.)

We should keep this in mind in the developing of our theology and doctrine. It is not wise to base a doctrinal tenet only on a poetic passage. The poetry should illustrate and amplify the doctrinal point that is presented elsewhere.

All poetry has a common characteristic in *vividness of expression*. Figurative language and a wide usage of figures of speech constitute one of the chief qualities of the poetic form. In that same 29th psalm, where the Lord makes the cedars of Lebanon to "skip like a calf," we have a use of poetic imagery that beautifully captures the effect of a tremendous windstorm on the mountainside.

But Hebrew poetry has some patterns that are quite different from what we expect. In English we know that poetry has the two qualities of rhythm and rhyme. There are various meters and patterns, but some type of rhyme and rhythm is typical. (Of course contemporary blank verse does away with these and depends almost exclusively on feeling and vividness of expression.)

Hebrew poetry, in contrast, uses a technique known as *parallelism of thought* as its basic characteristic. While there is some rhythm in the original text, this is largely incidental. The parallelisms are the important factors to observe. One might think of them as "thought rhythms" of a sort. There are three basic categories with certain variations possible.

(1) The first type may be called *synonymous parallelism*.[2] Here the psalmist says something and then repeats his thought in different words. Note the repetition in the following verse:

> But his delight is in the law of the Lord,
> And in His law he meditates day and night.[3]

Here one can readily see that the phrase "the law of the Lord" means the same as "His law" and the thought of delighting in the law is picked up by the fact that he meditates in the law "day and night." It might be helpful to suggest that one of the values of recognizing parallelisms is to understand more clearly the mind of the poet. We see that the thought here is not that the righteous man delights to *own* the law, but he delights to *meditate* in the law.

Various subtypes of synonymous parallelisms will be observed. There may be only the repetition of a portion of the initial statement. In the case of an extended parallelism, one part may be repeated while the second part is enlarged upon. These varieties are simply suggested with the realization that the serious student will readily observe them in the text.

(2) The second basic type of parallelism might be called *antithetic parallelism*. Here the poet does not *repeat* the thought, but *reverses* it. Note the following verse:

> For the Lord knows the way of the righteous,
> but the way of the wicked will perish.[4]

It can be seen immediately that "the way of the righteous" and "the way of the wicked" are opposites. This, plus the use of the common adversative "but," establishes the form as an antithetic parallelism. Then the student can see that, in the opinion of the poet, the opposite of being known by the Lord is to "perish."

(3) Finally, there is a very flexible type of parallelism known as *synthetic parallelism*. Here, as the name implies, the poet neither repeats nor reverses his thought, but *develops* it. The key to this type is progression of thought. We continue to look to Psalm 1 for our example. Note verse 1:

> How blessed is the man who does not walk in the
>   counsel of the wicked,
> Nor stand in the path of sinners,
> Nor sit in the seat of scoffers!

Note the progression here evidenced in the sequence of verbs "walk," "stand," "sit." The poet is seeking to get us to see the progression of association. If we begin to follow the advice of wicked people, we will soon be sitting in their company.

Perhaps a look at verse 3 of the same psalm will also help:

> And he will be like a tree firmly planted by streams
>   of water,
> Which yields its fruit in its season,
> And its leaf does not wither:
> And in whatever he does, he prospers.

Note that the first three lines constitute a typical synthetic parallelism; there is obvious progression from planting to fruit bearing and continuous foliage. The fourth line, however, presents an interesting variation. It is actually in synonymous parallel with all of the first three lines!

This flexibility is to be noted in all of Hebrew poetry. The poet does not feel bound to follow any fixed pattern. Psalm 1 reveals three synonymous parallelisms, two antithetic parallelisms, and two synthetic parallelisms. Other psalms will use only one type; there are numerous variations, etc. There is a freedom of expression that is exhilarating to observe.

Occasionally the psalmist elects to restrict himself to a more rigid format. One example is Psalm 119, which is a perfect acrostic. Here the psalmist, using all of the types of parallelisms, has produced a masterpiece of form. Each paragraph begins with a separate letter of the Hebrew alphabet, and within any given paragraph each line of the original text begins with the same letter! At the same time, all but four of the 176 verses in the psalm specifically refer to the Word of the Lord!

In addition to the structural patterns, it is well to note that there is a *concreteness* about Hebrew poetry. Rarely do you have vague, theoretical, and philosophical ideas expressed. In the psalms where the poet is anxious for the Lord's enemies (and his own) to be defeated, he is very specific about what he thinks the Lord should do. Consider Psalm 10:15:

> Break the arm of the wicked and the evildoer,

or Psalm 58:6:

> O God, shatter their teeth in their mouth.

There is a challenging honesty in this literature that makes us feel a kinship with the poet. Perhaps this is one of the reasons why the psalms have such a universal appeal to the people of God.

A correct appreciation of these characteristics will prove invaluable in a study of Hebrew poetry. If we do not make the effort to identify the parallelisms, we will miss much of what the poet is saying and remain unmoved by the emotion that motivated the writing of the psalm in the first place.

2. The Parables

The second type of biblical literature to which we should give some attention is the *parable*. We are most accustomed to this form in the ministry of the Lord Jesus, but it does occur elsewhere in the Scriptures.[5] There are several things that we should note.

(1) The parable is a story with a *purpose*. Jesus indicated that He taught in parables so that those who were not believers could not understand what He was saying.[6] Each parable, then, has a specific truth to communicate to those who believe. It is very important to determine the purpose of the given parable as one seeks to understand it.

(2) The parable is a *true-to-life* story that communicates a spiritual truth. It is not that the story necessarily actually happened, but that all of the factors are real and potentially possible so that it could have happened. It is important to remember this when reading the fascinating account of the rich man and Lazarus, the beggar.[7] While the event may not have actually happened, yet we know that if this is a parable, all of the details are true to life; therefore, Jesus was giving us insights about Hades and Paradise that we don't find elsewhere.

(3) The parable is a story, complete in itself, that is told to *parallel a spiritual truth*. The word parable comes from two Greek words *para*, meaning "alongside of," and *ballo*, meaning "to throw." It refers to "something thrown alongside" of something else, as the drawing of a line in parallel with another line. The only connection between the parable and the spiritual truth is in the explanation of the teacher or faith of the hearer, or both.

(4) Basically a parable is told to *communicate one spiritual truth.* The greatest disservice is done to the Word of God when we try to wrest and twist and squeeze the parables to see all kinds of hidden and symbolic meanings in them.

How then does one go about studying a parable? He first studies it *internally*, as discussed throughout this work, to insure that he understands the meaning and force of terms and structure. But then he seeks to determine what is the primary truth that it is seeking to communicate. While there may be secondary truths implicit in the story, these are not to be distorted or expanded out of proportion.

It is helpful to examine carefully those parables which Jesus tells and follows up with interpretation. Consider, for example, His presentation of the parable of the Soils and its interpretation.[8] This is one of the best known of the parables. Although it is usually referred to as the parable of the Sower, one can see that the important factor is the variety of the soils. Jesus, by means of this story, reveals to His disciples that when they preach, there will be four kinds of people who will hear them. The servant of the Lord should not get discouraged when only a small proportion of those to whom he ministers responds.

Seek to discover the purpose in giving the parable; isolate its primary truth; apply that truth to your own heart and to others.

3. Prophecy

One other type of biblical literature that should be discussed is *prophecy*. A large proportion of the Word has come down to us through the ministry of this fascinating group of men known as the prophets. The word means "one who speaks for another."

These men were God's spokesmen; each one served as the Lord's mouthpiece to his given culture and era. Much of his task was to warn of that which lay in the future, but often his function was to denounce the evil of the present.

In studying prophecy we accept by faith the fact that God is able to reveal the future if He so wishes. We are not disturbed when we see the prophet naming Cyrus as the deliverer of the people from Exile hundreds of years before Cyrus lived! [9] The skeptic says this is impossible and therefore seeks to find some author who knew Cyrus and inserted his name several centuries after the book was written. But we know it is simply another evidence of the greatness of our God!

A second factor in studying prophecy is to remember what has been called "The Law of Double Reference." That is, the prophet is speaking a message that has pertinence to his own day and also has a clear message for the future. As an example, in Isaiah 7 God tells King Ahaz to ask for a sign; the king, in his sullen disobedience, refuses. Whereupon the Lord through his prophet says:

> Therefore the Lord Himself will give you a sign: Behold, a virgin will be with child and bear a son, and she will call His name Immanuel. He will eat curds and honey at the time He knows enough to refuse evil and choose good. For before the boy will know enough to refuse evil and choose good, the land whose two kings you dread will be forsaken.[10]

Notice that this message spoke clearly to Ahaz' day. Before a boy born that year would be old enough to discern good and evil, God would deliver Judah from the oppression of her enemies. But the prophet was saying far more than this: "Behold a *virgin* will be with child . . . " Here he was looking

down the centuries and speaking of the great birth
of our Lord Jesus Christ. The same message had
two points of application, that is, a "double reference.
In studying prophecy one should always be alert
to this characteristic.[11]

The most difficult type of prophetic literature to
deal with is *apocalyptic* literature. The word comes
from the Greek and is related to the verb meaning
"to uncover." Therefore it has to do with revelation.
The final book of the New Testament is often referred
to as the Apocalypse of John. Here is a type of
literature that the Holy Spirit inspired John and certain of the prophets (especially Daniel, Zechariah
and Ezekiel) to utilize.

In contrast to other prophetic literature that most
often deals with Judah, Israel, or their contemporary
nations, apocalyptic literature deals with history in
the broadest sweep. The messianic hope is seen to
have worldwide significance: "The kingdom of the
world has become the kingdom of our Lord and of
His Christ; and He will reign forever and ever." [12]

This type of literature is characterized by visions
and angelic messengers. It uses a great deal of symbolic language, sometimes with angelic interpretation of the symbols, often with no clear key supplied.

The Bible student must approach the interpretation of apocalyptic literature with caution, humility,
reverence and patience. He must ask himself, "What
is the *main* teaching here?" One can readily become
lost in the curious details and succumb to the temptation of "private interpretation." [13]

Each symbol must be carefully isolated and studied. Are there other places in the Word where the
symbol is used? Can the comparative study of the
various uses help in understanding its use in the
present instance? Remember that a symbol is used

because there is some point of analogy that is important. Seek to discover what the analogy is that the author is stressing.

Consider, for example, the great vision of the throne-room of God described in Revelation 4! Notice verse 5. "And there were seven lamps of fire burning before the throne, which are the seven Spirits of God." How are we to interpret this? Are there multiple Spirits of God? Our knowledge of other scriptural teaching reminds us that the Spirit of God is a person, the Third Person of the Trinity. What, then, are we to conclude from this? Obviously we must wrestle with two symbols: "lamps of fire" and the number "seven." The analogy of fire is clear, indicating purification, power, light, heat, etc. The lamp can indicate source, while the number seven is the number of perfection. Therefore, we conclude that John is describing symbolically the perfect purifying ministry of the Spirit of God with its source at the very throne of God.

As we seek to put our interpretation to the test, we note the phrase in Revelation 5:6 where John describes "a Lamb standing, as if slain, having seven horns and *seven eyes, which are the seven Spirits of God*, sent out into all the earth." Again we see the emphases on the perfection ("seven") of the ministry of the Holy Spirit, with the added thought of His ministry throughout the earth.

Carefully, thoughtfully, prayerfully we compare each passage and seek to see the analogy of the symbol. Keep in mind that whatever you see in a symbol in apocalyptic literature must be in perfect harmony with what is taught, perhaps more clearly, in other literary patterns in the Scriptures. The Word of God is perfectly consistent within itself.

Care must, of course, be given to the reverent

acceptance of any interpretation within the passage itself. Often the prophet asks, "What does this mean?" Occasionally, the angel asks the prophet questions,[14] which the angel then proceeds to answer. The answers to these questions should be given very careful study.

The need for caution can be seen readily when one considers that many of the cults that spring up to delude people and lead them away from the Lord Jesus find their initial impetus in a distorted interpretation of apocalyptic literature.

Difficult as it may seem, we must always remember that the Bible has been given to us so that we might know what the Lord desires to reveal to us. The Lord is seeking to teach us to see the broad sweep of His program for men, and to trust Him for the details.

CHAPTER 9

Other Methods

Occasionally when students come to the end of a course in inductive Bible study such as we have discussed in this work, they ask the question, "What other ways or methods are there?" One suspects that they have a desire to find an easier way to accomplish the same end. It is the firm conviction of the author that the steps developed in the preceding pages provide the guidelines for coming to grips with the Word personally and with maximum spiritual benefit. It enables one not only to *know* the Word of God, but also to *love* the Word of God.

Other methods have been used in the past and are being used at present. Let us look at a few of those.

(1) *Allegorical interpretation.* Here the student assumes that the literal meaning of the passage is the least important thing; he searches for the key to some higher meaning. The ancient church father Origen was the first to do this, but many have followed him since. He suggested that all Scripture had three meanings, corresponding to the human body, soul and spirit. It was the so-called spiritual meaning that was most important. Of course, with this method

a gifted teacher can persuade his followers that the Scriptures mean whatever he wants them to mean. The cultist twists the Scriptures to his own interest and desire, supplying his own key to understanding them.[1]

(2) *Authoritative-liturgical interpretation.* Here the church tells the individual what the Scriptures mean. There is an 'official' interpretation that each member of the church is expected to accept and propagate. There is no need for careful study on your own. Just learn the doctrines of the church and let others do your studying for you.

(3) *Dogmatic interpretation.* This is somewhat related to the preceding one, but different in the sense that the authoritative Bible teacher takes the place of the church. He may indeed use the *grammatico-historical* approach,[2] which is such an integral part of personal Bible study, but he then expects the faithful to accept what *he* says and what *he* sees as the final interpretation. This is a comfortable type of interpretation because it requires little independent thinking. Many students prefer this easy way, and actually express disappointment when a professor does not tell them, "This is the outline! This is the teaching!"

(4) *Analysis-synthesis.* This is the method used in the more traditional approaches to hermeneutics. *Analysis* refers to breaking down the whole book into its component parts; *synthesis* refers to the reconstructing of the parts back into the whole. The student will readily see that this is the method advocated in this book for personal Bible study. We too have progressed first from the whole to the parts, and then from the parts to the whole. The only objection that we raise to this approach is that what the instructor has discovered is often taken to be the

finished product. In other words, the *instructor* does the analysis and the synthesis while the *students* take notes on what he says the passage teaches.

This particular approach is popular with students because it is the professor who does the hard work. All of the background study, the research, the interpretation of symbols, etc., is already done. The material is fed to the students in a predigested form.

The problem is that what comes easily also goes easily. We can record the results of the professor's study in our notebooks without becoming really vitally involved with it at all. We can even reproduce it beautifully on an examination, but when the course is over we can recall very little. In *personal* Bible study, by way of contrast, we remember what we have found because we did the work ourselves.

(5) *Doctrinal studies.* There is, of course, a place for this kind of study. One traces the biblical teaching concerning a specific doctrine right through the Scriptures in order to see what the Word has to say about it. This is the only way to be sure we have sound doctrine. The only note of caution to be sounded here is that one must be sure that his doctrinal teaching comes out of the Word, and not the other way around. That is, beware lest your desire to propagate a particular doctrine causes you to distort the scripture in order to force it into a doctrinal mold.

(6) *Word studies.* This is similar to the preceding method. One takes a particular word and studies its use throughout the Scriptures. One fine evangelical pastor has used this method for many years as the basis of his preaching and writing.[3] Just as long as this method is used as a supplement to basic inductive study, it has genuine value. Obviously, if it were the only method employed, the student would have little knowledge of the total teaching of the

Scriptures or of the individual books of the Bible.

(7) *Biographical studies.* This is another valuable supplementary method of studying. Take the life of a biblical character and very carefully study every passage in the Scriptures that applies to him. This would involve not only the historical passages that describe his life, but also every reference made to him in other sections of the Word. This is not only rewarding in the study of the great men, such as Moses, Abraham, Jacob, etc., but it can provide great insights into some of the lesser personalities of the Bible. Much can be gained by searching out every reference to Melchizedech, Balaam, Enoch, etc.

There may be other detailed methods that could be used in a supplementary manner. Naturally any method that enables us to grasp the Word better and understand the truths of God more fully is to be used in its proper place. The appeal of the present work is that good, solid, inductive book-by-book study is the basic method which should be used if we wish to know and use the Word of God.

The time has come to conclude this work. Other things could be said; illustrations could be given; exhortations could be multiplied. Suffice it to say that this work has been done prayerfully with the earnest desire that young men and women will come to love the Word of God as their most precious possession. This will only happen as they realize that it is a personal message from the heart of God to them; since that is so, every effort expended in the study of God's Word will be worthwhile.

Mr. Traina, in his section on observation, reminds his readers that in order to do the task correctly, they must have three requirements: The will to do it, exactness in their work, and persistence to stay with the task until it is done.[4] No more appropriate words could be used with which to end this manual. He quotes the following poem by Clarence Edward Flynn:

Peering into the mists of gray
That shroud the surface of the bay,
Nothing I see except a veil
Of fog surrounding every sail.
Then suddenly against a cape
A vast and silent form takes shape,
A great ship lies against the shore
Where nothing has appeared before.

Who sees a truth must often gaze
Into a fog for many days;
It may seem very sure to him
Nothing is there but mist-clouds dim.
Then, suddenly, his eyes will see
A shape where nothing used to be.
Discoveries are missed each day
By men who turn too soon away.[5]

The Student, the Fish, and Agassiz

by the Student

It was more than fifteen years ago that I entered the laboratory of Professor Agassiz and told him I had enrolled my name in the scientific school as a student of natural history. He asked me a few questions about my object in coming, my antecedents generally, the mode in which I afterwards proposed to use the knowledge I might acquire, and finally, whether I wished to study any special branch. To the latter I replied that while I wished to be well-grounded in all departments of zoology, I purposed to devote myself specially to insects.

"When do you wish to begin?" he asked.

"Now," I replied.

This seemed to please him, and with an energetic "Very well," he took from a shelf a huge jar of specimens in yellow alcohol.

"Take this fish," said he, "and look at it; we call it a Haemulon (pronounced Hem-yúlon); by and by I will ask what you have seen."

With that he left me, but in a moment returned with explicit instructions as to the care of the object entrusted to me.

"No man is fit to be a naturalist," said he, "who does not know how to take care of specimens."

I was to keep the fish before me in a tin tray, and occasionally moisten the surface with alcohol from the jar, always taking care to replace the stopper tightly. Those were not the days of ground glass stoppers and elegantly shaped exhibition jars; all the old students will recall the huge, neckless glass bottles and their leaky, wax-be-smeared corks, half eaten by insects and begrimed with cellar dust. Entomology was a cleaner science than ichthyology, but the example of the professor who had unhesitatingly plunged to the bottom of the jar to produce the fish was infectious; and though this alcohol had "a very ancient and fishlike smell," I really dared not show any aversion within these sacred precincts, and treated the alcohol as though it were pure water. Still I was con-scious of a passing feeling of disappointment, for gazing at a fish did not commend itself to an ardent entomologist. My friends at home, too, were annoyed when they discov-ered that no amount of Eau de Cologne would drown the perfume which haunted me like a shadow.

In ten minutes I had seen all that could be seen in that fish, and started in search of the professor who had, however, left the museum; and when I returned, after lingering over some of the odd animals stored in the upper apartment, I found my specimen to be dry all over. I dashed the fluid over the fish as if to resuscitate it from a fainting spell, and looked with anxiety for a return of the normal, sloppy appearance. This little excitement over, nothing was to be done but return to a steadfast gaze at my mute companion. Half an hour passed, an hour, another hour; the fish began to look loathsome. I turned it over and around, looked it in the face—ghastly; I looked at it from behind, beneath, above, sideways, at a three-quarters' view—just as ghastly. I was in despair. At an early hour I concluded that lunch was necessary; so with infinite relief, I carefully replaced the fish in the jar, and for an hour I was free.

On my return, I learned that Professor Agassiz had been at the museum, but had gone and would not return for several hours. My fellow students were too busy to

be disturbed by continued conversation. Slowly I drew forth
that hideous fish, and with a feeling of desperation looked
at it again. I might not use a magnifying glass; instruments
of all kinds were interdicted. My two hands, my two eyes,
and the fish—it seemed a most limited field. I pushed
my fingers down its throat to see how sharp its teeth were.
I began to count the scales in the different rows until
I was convinced that that was nonsense. At last a
happy thought struck me—I would draw the fish—and
now with surprise I began to discover new features in
the creature. Just then the professor returned.

"That is right," said he, "a pencil is one of the best
eyes. I am glad to notice, too, that you keep your specimen
wet and your bottle corked." With these encouraging words
he added, "Well, what is it like?"

He listened attentively to my brief rehearsal of the structure of parts whose names were still unknown to me: the
fringed gill—arches and movable operculum; the pores
of the head, fleshly lips, and lidless eyes; the lateral line,
the spinous fin, and forked tail; the compressed and arched
body.

When I had finished, he waited as if expecting more,
and then, with an air of disappointment, he said, "You
have not looked very carefully." He continued, more
earnestly, "You haven't seen one of the most conspicuous
features of the animal, which is as plainly before your
eyes as the fish itself. Look again! look again!" and he
left me to my misery.

I was piqued; I was mortified. Still more of that
wretched fish? But now I set myself to the task with
a will, and discovered one new thing after another, until
I saw how just the professor's criticism had been.

The afternoon passed quickly, and then, towards its
close, the professor inquired, "Do you see it yet?"

"No," I replied, "I am certain I do not, but I see how
little I saw before."

"That is next best," said he earnestly, "but I won't
hear you now; put away your fish and go home; perhaps
you will be ready with a better answer in the morning.

I will examine you then, before you look at the fish."

This was disconcerting. Not only must I think of my fish all night, studying, without the object before me, what this unknown but most visible feature might be, but also, without reviewing my new discoveries, I must give an exact account of them the next day. I had a bad memory; so I walked home by Charles River in a distracted state, with my perplexities.

The cordial greeting from the professor the next morning was reassuring. Here was a man who seemed to be quite as anxious as I that I should see for myself what he saw.

"Do you perhaps mean," I asked, "that the fish has symmetrical sides with paired organs?"

His thoroughly pleased, "Of course, of course!" repaid the wakeful hours of the previous night. After he had discoursed most happily and enthusiastically, as he always did, upon the importance of this point, I ventured to ask what I should do next.

"Oh, look at your fish!" he said, and then left me again to my own devices. In a little more than an hour he returned and heard my new catalogue.

"That is good, that is good!" he repeated, "but that is not all; go on." And so, for three long days he placed that fish before my eyes, forbidding me to look at anything else, or to use any artificial aid. "Look, look, look," was his repeated injunction.

This was the best entomological lesson I ever had, a lesson whose influence has extended to the details of every subsequent study. It was a legacy the professor has left to me, as he left it to many others, a legacy of inestimable value, which we could not buy, with which we cannot part.

A year afterwards, some of us were amusing ourselves with chalking outlandish beasts upon the blackboard. We drew prancing starfishes; frogs in mortal combat; hydro-headed worms; stately crawfishes standing on their tails, bearing aloft umbrellas; and grotesque fishes with gaping mouths and staring eyes. The professor came in shortly after, and was as much amused as any at our experiments. He looked at the fishes.

"Haemulons, every one of them," he said, "Mr.___ drew them."

True; and to this day, if I attempt to draw a fish, I can draw nothing but Haemulons.

The fourth day a second fish of the same group was placed beside the first, and I was bidden to point out the resemblances and difference between the two; another and another followed, until the entire family lay before me, and a whole legion of jars covered the table and surrounding shelves. The odor had become a pleasant perfume, and even now the sight of an old, six-inch, worm-eaten cork brings fragrant memories!

The whole group of Haemulons was thus brought into view; and whether engaged upon the dissection of the internal organs, preparation and examination of the bony framework, or the description of the various parts, Agassiz's training in the method of observing facts and their orderly arrangement, was ever accompanied by the urgent exhortation not to be content with them.

"Facts are stupid things," he would say, "until brought into connection with some general law."

At the end of eight months, it was almost with reluctance that I left these friends and turned to insects; but what I gained by this outside experience has been of greater value than years of later investigation in my favorite groups.

—Appendix American Poems (probably Boston: Houghton, Osgood and Co. 1880). From *Independent Bible Study* by Irving L. Jensen. Copyright © 1963 by Moody Press, Moody Bible Institute of Chicago. Used by permission.

NOTES

All scripture references, unless otherwise noted, are taken from the *New American Standard Bible* (NASB), published by Creation House, Carol Stream, Illinois.

CHAPTER 1

1. The phrase *methodical inductive Bible study* follows the very significant work of Professor Robert A. Traina, Asbury Theological Seminary, Wilmore, Kentucky.

2. Quoted in Robert A. Traina, *Methodical Bible Study* (privately published in 1952), p. 5.

3. *Ibid.*

CHAPTER 2

1. Jill Morgan, *This Was His Faith* (Westwood, N.J.: Fleming H. Revell, 1952), p. 24 (emphasis added).

2. Don M. Wagner, *The Expository Method of G. Campbell Morgan* (Westwood, N. J.: Revell, 1957), p. 51.

3. Mortimer J. Adler, *How to Read a Book* (New York: Simon and Schuster, 1940), p. 124.

CHAPTER 3

1. Adler, *op. cit.*, p. 187.

2. I am indebted for this particular suggestion to the work of Irving L. Jensen, *Independent Bible Study* (Chicago: Moody Press, 1963), p. 53ff.

3. For further development, see Traina, *op. cit.*, pp. 50-52.

4. I acknowledge my debt here to Merrill F. Unger, *Principles of Expository Preaching* (Grand Rapids: Zondervan Publishing House, 1955), pp. 175-185.

CHAPTER 4

1. Cf. Matt. 18:3.

2. Quoted in Traina, *op. cit.*, p. 75.

3. Luke 3:1.

4. See the article entitled, "Time," *International Standard Bible Encyclopedia* (Chicago: Howard-Severance Co., 1925), 5:2982.

5. Rom. 8:28 (cf. KJV with NASB).

6. John 8:31-32.

7. John 3:9.

8. See Traina, *op. cit.*, pp. 109-110, for the use of these terms. Mr. Traina refers to these questions as *subordinate* questions.

9. Mr. Traina calls the *why* question *rational* and the *what* question *definitive*. The two questions are *basic* questions. See *op. cit.*, p. 99.

10. Heb. 4:12.

11. Mr. Traina refers to this question as the *implicational* question. See *op. cit.*, p. 99.

12. Mr. Traina calls this the *atmosphere* of the passage. See *op. cit.*, p. 104.

13. Rom. 3:4.

CHAPTER 5

1. Mark 2:4; see also Luke 5:19.

2. John 19:40.

3. Luke 10:30.

4. See Edersheim, *The Life and Times of Jesus the Messiah* (Grand Rapids: Eerdmans), 2:349.

5. Cf. John 2:13; 5:1, et al.

6. One of the best treatments of charting of which the

author is aware is contained in the book by Irving L. Jensen, *op. cit.* This work has many helpful suggestions for inductive study.

7. John 11:38 ff.

8. Cf. John 20:7.

CHAPTER 6

1. Irving Wallace, *The Word* (New York: Simon and Schuster, 1972), p. 150.

2. Matt. 14:28-31.

3. Lloyd Douglas, *The Robe* (New York: Houghton Mifflin Co., 1942), p. 309 (emphasis added).

4. 2 Kings 6:1-7.

5. Ps. 116:13.

6. Matt. 24:35.

7. This particular step is identified by Mr. Traina as *correlation.* See Traina, *op. cit.*, pp. 223-227.

8. Mark 6:39.

9. Cf. Num. 15:5; 28:7

10. Franz Delitzsch, *Biblical Commentary on the Psalms* (London: Hodder and Stoughton, 1889), p. 202.

11. Kenneth S. Wuest, *Studies in the Vocabulary of the Greek New Testament* (Grand Rapids: Wm. B. Eerdmans, 1945). Many of the other works by Mr. Wuest are also very helpful and rewarding.

CHAPTER 7

1. Heb. 4:12-13.

2. Gal. 6:14.

3. 2 Tim. 3:16-17.

4. Acts 4:32.

5. Cf. 1 John 3:17.

6. Matt. 28:18-20.

7. 1 Cor. 14:34.

8. Heb. 12:6.

9. Acts 7:52.

10. Mark 16:15-16.

11. Jer. 20:9.

CHAPTER 8

1. 2 Cor. 4:2.

2. Any discussion of Hebrew poetry must acknowledge a debt to the epoch-making work of Bishop Robert Lowth (d. 1787) who first discovered this key to biblical poetry. The basic terms discussed here were originally suggested by him.

3. Ps. 1:2.

4. Ps. 1:6.

5. Cf. Ezek. 17, et al. Note that most of Jesus' parables dealt with *human* experience, but nature plays a part as well.

6. See Mark 4:11, 12.

7. Luke 16:19-31.

8. Matt. 13:3-23; Mark 4:3-20; Luke 8:5-15.

9. Isa. 44:28; 45:1.

10. Isa. 7:14-16.

11. A further illustration of this can be seen in Ezekiel 28, where the prophet speaks of the downfall both of the king of Tyre and of Satan, who inspires the wicked king.

12. Rev. 11:15.

13. 2 Pet. 1:20 (AV).

14. See, for example, Rev. 7:13, 14; Ezek. 37:3.

CHAPTER 9

1. Consider Mary Baker Eddy's book, *Science and Health with a Key to the Scriptures.*

2. The *grammatico-historical* approach is a term used for the type of Bible study that carefully considers word usages in their historical setting. This can be seen to lie at the heart of personal Bible study. We are concerned that we wrestle with every word in its grammatical force and also that we have a thorough background and understanding of the historical period in which it was written.

3. The pastor referred to is the Rev. Mr. Leslie B. Flynn, pastor of the Grace Conservative Baptist Church, Nanuet, N.Y. His books are very worthwhile. See especially, *Did*

I Say That? (Nashville: Broadman Press, 1959), and *Serve Him With Mirth* (Grand Rapids: Zondervan, 1960).

4. Traina, *op. cit.,* pp. 32-33.

5. *Ibid.,* p. 33.

BIBLIOGRAPHY

(Many of the basic tools cited in chapter 5 are not repeated here. Full bibliographic data will be found in the text or the notes of that chapter.)

A. Books written from the perspective of inductive study of the Scriptures:

Hollingsworth, Jane. *Discovering Mark*. Chicago: Inter-Varsity Press, 1950.

Jensen, Irving L. *Independent Bible Study*. Chicago: Moody Press, 1963.

Kuist, Howard Tillman. *These Words upon Thy Heart*. Richmond: John Knox Press, 1947.

Richards, Lawrence O. *Creative Bible Study*. Grand Rapids: Zondervan Publishing House, 1971.

(This work is designed to guide in group study and sharing of discoveries in the Word. It is not strictly following the methodology advocated in the present work, but it does emphasize subjective exposure and self-discovery in the Scriptures.)

Traina, Robert A. *Methodical Bible Study*. Privately published, 1952.

Wald, Oletta. *The Joy of Discovery*. Minneapolis: Bible Banner Press, 1956.

B. Other books in the general field of Hermeneutics:

Berkhof, Louis. *Principles of Biblical Interpretation*. Grand Rapids: Baker Book House, 1957.

Dungan, Prof. D. R. *Hermeneutics, A Text-Book*. Cincinnati: Standard Pub. House, n.d.

Evans, William. *The Book Method of Bible Study*. Chicago: Bible Institute Colportage Association, 1915.

Keiper, Ralph L. *How to Study Your Bible*. Philadelphia: The Evangelistic Foundation, 1961.

Rees, Tom. *Break-Through*. Waco, Texas: Word Books, 1970. (Guidance for conducting "Bible Cell-groups")

Ridout, S. *How to Study the Bible*. New York: Loizeaux Brothers, n.d.

Smith, Wilbur M. *Profitable Bible Study*. rev. ed. Boston: W. A. Wilde Co., 1953.

Terry, Milton S. *Biblical Hermeneutics*. Grand Rapids: Zondervan Pub. House, n.d.

Thomas, W. H. Griffith. *Methods of Bible Study*. Chicago: Moody Press, 1926.

Torrey, R. A. *How to Study the Bible for Greatest Profit*. New York: Fleming H. Revell, 1896.

Vos, Howard. *Effective Bible Study*. Grand Rapids: Zondervan, 1956.

C. Other works cited or helpful:

Adler, Mortimer J. *How to Read a Book*. New York: Simon and Schuster, 1940.

Danker, Frederick W. *Multipurpose Tools for Bible Study*. St. Louis: Concordia Pub. House, 1960.

Edersheim, Alfred. *The Life and Times of Jesus the Messiah*. Two volumes, Grand Rapids: Wm. B. Eerdsmans, 1945.

_____ *The Temple*: Its Ministry and Services. Grand Rapids: Wm. B. Eerdsmans, 1954.

_____ *Sketches of Jewish Social Life*. Grand Rapids: Wm. B. Eerdmans, 1953.

Flynn, Leslie B. *Did I Say That?* Nashville: Broadman Press, 1959.

_____ *Serve Him with Mirth*. Grand Rapids: Zondervan, 1960.

Morgan, Jill. *This Was His Faith*. Westwood, N.J.: Fleming H. Revell, 1952.

Oakes, John P. *Exploring Your Bible*. Grand Rapids: Zondervan Pub. House, 1960.

Unger, Merrill F. *Principles of Expository Preaching*. Grand Rapids: Zondervan Pub. House, 1955.

Wagner, Don M. *The Expository Method of G. Campbell Morgan*. Westwood, N.J.: Fleming H. Revell, 1957.

Wuest, Kenneth S. *Studies in the Vocabulary of the Greek N.T.* Grand Rapids: Wm. B. Eerdmans, 1945.

(Many of Mr. Wuest's books are very helpful to the English-speaking student.)

Young, Edward J. *Thy Word Is Truth*. Grand Rapids: Wm. B. Eerdmans Co., 1960.